SOURDOUGH

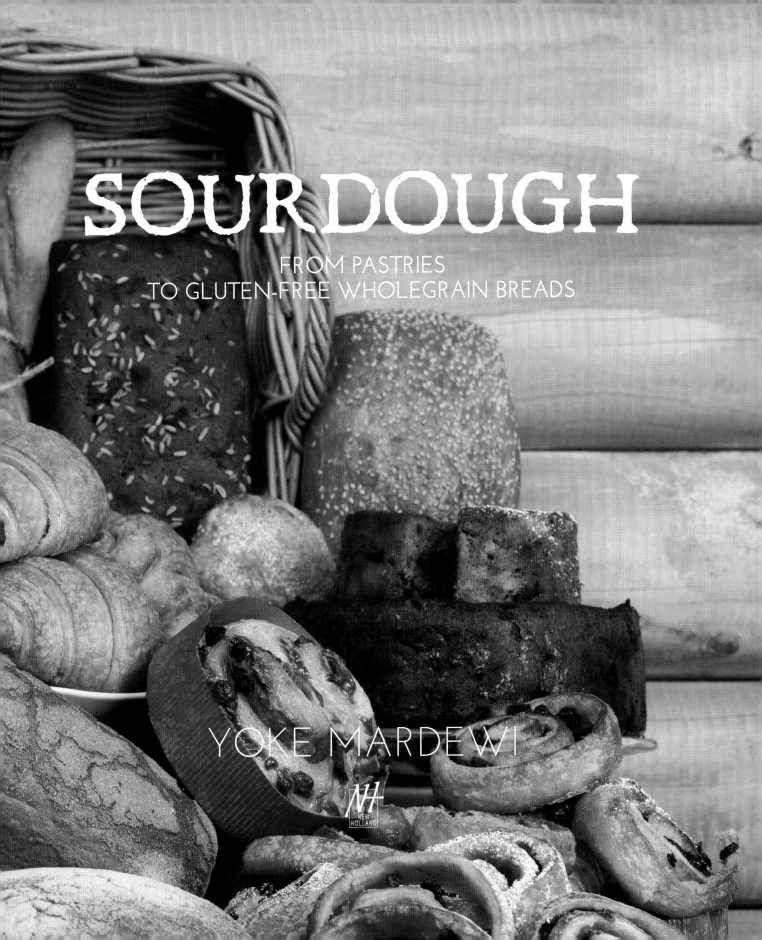

SOURDOUGH

FROM PASTRIES
TO GLUTEN-FREE WHOLEGRAIN BREADS

YOKE MARDEWI

NEW HOLLAND

to my daughter, Dechen,
the light of my life

CONTENTS

[Breadmaking is] one of those almost hypnotic businesses, like a dance from some ancient ceremony. It leaves you filled with one of the world's sweetest smells ... there is no chiropractic treatment, no yoga exercise, no hour of meditation in a music-throbbing chapel, that will leave you emptier of bad thoughts than this homely ceremony of making bread.

– M.F.K. FISHER, *THE ART OF EATING*

English Muffins

INTRODUCTION

This book has been a long, but extremely rewarding, journey from my previous book, *Wild Sourdough*. The journey has been full of highs and lows, excitements and disappointments—some experiences served as necessary stepping stones to the next level, others I had to leave behind. But nothing is ever wasted; even failures were an indispensable part of the process, just as in life itself.

One great example of this was, had I never experimented with creating heavy rye breads (50 per cent rye or more), the techniques for creating gluten-free sourdough wholegrain may never have been discovered. And yet rye and gluten-free sourdough behave very differently. There were days when I sat in tears after throwing away batch after batch of failed gluten-free loaves—but I vividly remember days when I beamed with an inner glow of utter ecstasy, because the recipes I created worked better than I had expected.

This book is intended to be completely different from my first book with new recipes and techniques, except for five recipes of basic sourdough, which I deliberately included to complete the scope of this book. There was no point in writing (or for you, readers, buying) another book that is just a different shade of the same colour. In order to do this, I have gone out on a limb and discovered a new world of sourdough croissants, pastries, gluten-free wholegrains, soft sourdough rolls and loaves, and more.

I have simplified some techniques, but I have also expanded the range and provided more explanations for the basics, including step-by-step instructions for creating and activating starters, both gluten (rye, wheat and spelt) and gluten-free.

For you eager novice bakers, I would encourage you to read the first few chapters preceeding the recipes. These will give you a basic understanding of the how and why of the ingredients and techniques used in the recipes. Remember, nothing is difficult—it is just practice, persistence and patience (oh ... if only the rest of our lives were as easy as sourdough bread making).

In my experience of teaching thousands of students, it is best to start by mastering one or two basic recipes, then go on to explore the more complex ones. There will be a time when suddenly all your efforts will just come together. Remember, our ancestors made sourdough breads for thousands of years without the advent of modern technology such as the electric oven, dough-kneading machine, filtered water, etc.

For me, sourdough bread making has been more than just the manual exercise of mixing flour with water. It is, more often than not, the 'pick-me-up' I need from life's lows. The act of making bread has never failed to lift my spirits, banish my bad thoughts and take me back to the space where I need to be.

'My hope is that, apart from making the most delicious and nourishing bread, the art of making sourdough bread will delight your soul, bring you joy and provide you a most enjoyable solace.'

rolls rising in a tin

GETTING STARTED

oat flour

wholemeal spelt

rye flour

white wheat flour

wholemeal wheat flour

atta flour

coarse semolina flour

Kamut flour

malted wheat

malted wheat flour

white spelt flour

Gluten Flours

INGREDIENTS

The ingredient list of sourdough is very short, because the only ingredients you need for making delicious and nourishing sourdough bread are flour, water and salt. No oil or sugar/honey is required, unless you are making special enriched or flavoured breads.

The history of wheat and coeliac disease

Here is a condensed history of wheat, which also examines the emergence of coeliac disease. My hope is that this will shed a little light on the different types of wheat (Triticum species) and its early wheat ancestors.

Early wheat came from the family of early grasses and belongs to the species, Triticum. These early wheat species are classified as diploid, because they have two sets of chromosomes in their DNA. Einkorn is an ancient diploid wheat, known to man as far back as 16 000BC, and it is still grown in some isolated areas of France, India, Italy, Turkey and Yugoslavia.

Einkorn was superseded by Emmer during the Bronze Age (10 000–4 000BC). This early diploid grass mixed with another diploid wild grass to produce Emmer. Emmer, therefore, contains four sets of chromosomes, and is classified by geneticists as Tetraploid.

From Emmer emerged two different groups of hexaploid wheat, with the addition of two more sets of wild grass chromosomes. These are spelt (T.spelta) and modern wheat (T.aestivum). Modern wheat (T.aestivum) was the preferred species for modern farming because the grain kernels thresh free of the hulls. Modern wheat was further hybridised to create higher gluten/protein, higher yields, more adaptability to harsher growing conditions and greater pest resistance.

Ancient wheats—Einkorn, Emmer and Spelt—require more of an effort to remove their hulls. Thanks to this unique characteristic, early wheat is unattractive to modern farming.

Recent findings from genome mapping seem to indicate that the culprit gene responsible for initiating toxic/allergic reactions in people with coeliac gene inheritance belongs to the last two sets of chromosomes added, which the hexaploid wheat acquired from its wild grass parent. It is now believed that both diploid (e. Einkorn), and tetraploid (Emmer, Kamut and some durum wheat) are free of this mischievous gene.

I do believe fast modern bread production is also responsible for the rise of coeliac disease. Our ancestors, who were eating and making slow-risen sourdough bread, were practically free from the disease. This is due to the lactobacilli's pre-digestion of gluten in proper (slow) sourdough fermentation. Just a decade ago, coeliac sufferers were a rare phenomena, occurring in one in every 2 500 people. This rate increased exponentially in the 1990's, when one in 130 people suffer from coeliac disease in the United States with almost as many sufferers elsewhere. However,

Gluten-free Flours

buckwheat flour

sorghum flour

tapioca/cassava flour

potato flour.

chia seeds

ground golden
lindseed.

brown rice flour

chestnut flour

quinoa flour

caution and medical supervision is advised when dealing with such a controversial and not well-understood disease such as coeliac.

Flour

Flour, being the major ingredient of your bread, is so vital to the taste. Use the best quality, freshest, unbleached flour you can afford, preferably organic/biodynamic. The bleaching process in flour, apart from its toxicity, destroys (oxidises) beta-carotenoids in the flour, causing the bread you make with it to be tasteless.

I always endeavour to find biodynamic or organic flours that are grown locally. It is not necessarily true that organic flours always taste better and produce better bread than non-organic counterparts, but for me it is important to look after our precious earth. Locally grown ingredients often mean fresher produce—highly important for wholemeal/wholegrain flours, which can go rancid very fast if not stored properly in a refrigerated or cool room.

The type of flour you use depends on what type of bread you would like to make. There is no such thing as the best flour, because everyone's taste is so different. With practice and experimentation you will develop the intuition to 'design' your very own favourite bread. My own preference for everyday bread is a 50/50 wheat and spelt sourdough bread (one being a wholemeal flour) or a 70 per cent unbleached white premium baker's flour and 30 per cent organic wholemeal spelt.

FLOUR CONTAINING GLUTEN

Wheat flour

Wheat flour is the most commonly used flour in bread making. Wheat flour used in bread-making will need a gluten (protein) content of more than 10g per 100g (or 10 per cent of the total weight). Bread made with wheat has good volume and a beautiful sweet, nutty flavour. In Australia, the average gluten content of organic wheat is around 10–11 per cent. Wholemeal flours have more gluten and fibres than white flours.

There are two types of proteins in gluten: gliadin and glutenin. It is believed that the culprit gene creating the coeliac reaction is found in gliadin and wheat gluten has more gliadin than spelt.

Spelt flour

Spelt, the ancient wheat, has been heralded lately as a better grain than wheat. There have been so many wheat intolerant people who have been advised to try spelt as an alternative. I believe it is a common misconception that spelt is somewhat different from wheat. As far as I know, spelt has a higher protein/gluten content than wheat, being around 14 per cent, even though spelt has a lower ratio of coeliac inducing gliadin.

Spelt gives the bread a reddish-brown colour and an appealing caramel-like flavour. You can substitute wheat for spelt or spelt for wheat interchangeably.

Kamut, semolina and durum flours

All these grains belong to the same family. However, these are the 'hard wheats', which are commonly known as durum wheat. They are best suited for making pasta. They are to be used sparingly (no more than 25–30 per cent of total flour) in bread making as they tend to produce a hard and dense bread, with a thick crust.

Kamut (also known in Australia as Egyptian Gold) has golden, coloured grains giving a beautiful golden colour in both the crumb and the crust. It adds nutty flavour and a crusty crust to bread. Semolina flour is made from durum wheat and has similar characteristics to kamut when added to bread.

Rye, oat and barley flours

These are low-gluten grains. Of the three grains, oat has the least gluten and rye has the most. Rye has another unfavourable quality in bread making: it contains a polysaccharide called pentosan, which forms a glue-like substance once it is mixed with water. Because we need water in bread making, bread made with a higher percentage of rye will be dense and heavy, with poor volume.

These low-gluten flours, therefore, are to be used sparingly in bread making (no more than 20 percent of total flour), unless you specifically want a very dense bread (popular in northern Europe). Rye and oats give a silkiness to any dough, and barley gives the ultimate sweetness. Used sparingly and intelligently, they add complexities and unique flavours and textures to bread. Rye works really well with caraway seeds as flavouring.

Due to many requests from readers of my previous book, *Wild Sourdough*, I have developed sourdough bread containing higher percentages of rye (50 per cent to 100 per cent rye). These rye-rich recipes are included for those readers who prefer to eat mostly rye bread.

GLUTEN-FREE FLOUR

Chickpea flour (gram, garbanzo or besan flour)

Chickpea flour is made from ground chickpeas. It is used in many countries on the Indian subcontinent. It is commonly used in gluten-free bread making and cooking as a thickener, egg-replacer and protein enricher. I have not used this in my gluten-free sourdough because I do not like the unpleasant 'bean smell' it gives to baked bread.

Brown rice flour

Brown rice flour is made from ground kernels of rice from which only the hull has been removed. It is used in my gluten-free sourdough starter because it ferments really well, giving an almost neutral-smelling starter. It acts as a bulker and the good news is it is readily available at reasonable cost. Brown rice flour is available from bread shops, health food shops, supermarkets and asian grocers (or you can grind your own from brown rice kernels).

Brown rice starter tends to separate readily after mixing—to prevent this, I add ground linseed (or linseed meal) to my brown rice starter.

I find brown rice based sourdough gluten-free bread will be more 'cakey' or heavier in its texture than any buckwheat-based sourdough bread. However, it has a milder flavour.

Buckwheat flour

Buckwheat flour comes from ground buckwheat seed. Buckwheat, despite its name, does not belong to the wheat family and it is not a grass either—it is related to rhubarb. The kernel is a triangular-shaped seed with a black shell. It is hulled and ground to produce fine flour. Buckwheat flour is silky and has an earthy smell. Some people find buckwheat's smell strong and its taste, bitter. However, if used in sourdough fermentation, these two problems are significantly reduced. I love both the taste and consistency of buckwheat—it gives my gluten-free wholegrain sourdough a lighter, spongier, 'bread-like' structure to its crumb.

As a starter, buckwheat ferments easily and produces a beautiful silky-smooth, spongy starter. Its texture is between a sponge cake batter and a melting ice-cream. To reduce the slight bitter taste, you can add a small amount of sweetener to any of the buckwheat recipes. In some recipes, I have also added neutral tasting and smelling sorghum flour into my buckwheat starter. The addition of sorghum substantially dilutes the strong taste and smell of buckwheat. Buckwheat flour is available from bread shops, health food shops and asian grocers.

Cassava flour (tapioca, manioc, yucca)

Cassava flour is the starch that is extracted from the root of the cassava plant, and ground into flour, which is used as a thickener. It can be used interchangeably with potato flour. Please make sure that your cassava flour does not contain any preservative. In Australia, cassava flour is often misleadingly sold as arrowroot flour. I avoid this 'false' arrowroot flour because it has a sulphur-based preservative. Cassava flour is available from most asian grocers.

Cornflour (cornstarch)

I have included cornflour in this section because I want you to understand why I do not use this in any of my recipes! I have three reasons:

- Corn is the most widely used cereal grain in the world and it is also the most genetically modified.
- It is often confused with 'cornflour made from wheat starch' (often called 'wheaten cornflour'), which is unsuitable for people with gluten intolerance.
- It has no nutritional value whatsoever.

While cornflour does create lightness to bread and cakes, potato flour and cassava flour are excellent substitutes, with no genetically modified genes and more nutrients than corn starches.

Potato flour and potato starch flour

It is important to make the distinction between potato flour and potato starch flour. Potato flour is made from ground whole potato. It retains both the potato flavour and vitamins/minerals. It makes the gluten-free loaf lighter in texture, in my gluten-free sourdough recipes. You can substitute cassava/tapioca flour. Potato flour is available from health food shops, eastern european and asian grocers.

Potato starch flour or potato starch is prepared from cooked potatoes that are washed of all fibres, until only the starch remains. Potato starch is devoid of any nutrients—it is just pure starch. Avoid this if you can.

Quinoa flour

Quinoa flour is ground from quinoa seeds. Quinoa is not a cereal grain or a grass seed, and is related to spinach and amaranth. It has a mild, nutty flavour and very high in protein. I prefer to grind my own quinoa flour (see Flaxseed), because quinoa seeds have a coating of bitter-tasting saponin (soap-like substance), which is toxic and unpalatable. It is very hard to know whether quinoa seeds or flour sold commercially have been processed to remove this coating.

To make quinoa flour, you first need to rinse quinoa seeds thoroughly to remove this soapy substance, running them a few times under running water. Soak your seeds for about 4 to 6 hours, then rinse the seeds again and dry them under a hot sun, in a dehydrator or in a low oven. Once dried, you can grind your quinoa seeds into flour. It is better for you and cheaper to grind/make your own quinoa flour.

Flaxseed or linseed meal (ground flax/linseed)

Flaxseed or linseed meal is made from whole flax/linseeds—but for freshness, it is better to buy refrigerated flax/linseed and grind your own. Use your coffee grinder to grind your linseed, but only do small amounts at a time to prevent making an oily paste. Linseed meal goes rancid quickly, especially if it is not kept refrigerated. This seed contains very high levels of Omega 3. There are two types of linseed, brown or golden yellow. I prefer the look and taste of Australian/locally-grown golden yellow linseed.

Chia seeds

Chia seeds have gained its popularity in Australia recently—so much so that Australia is now the largest grower of chia seeds in the world! Chia seeds are incredibly rich (about 30 per cent of its weight) in both Omega 3 and 6 content, which make them very unique (I like to add chia gel to my smoothie and yoghurt drinks). Chia seeds are harvested from a species of flowering plant in the mint family, native to South America.

To use chia seeds, they need to be soaked in water to produce a chia gel which is then used in making gluten-free sourdough breads. Chia gel adds body and behaves somewhat like a glue to replace gluten or egg-white in gluten-free bread products. Be careful, as too much chia gel will make your gluten-free sourdough bread heavy, gluggy and cake-like.

Chestnut flour

The best quality chestnut flour is made from freeze-dried chestnuts. This type of chestnut flour has an intense fresh chestnut flavour and, as it is made using peeled chestnuts, there is no contamination from the inner skin of the chestnut that so often appears in other chestnut flours. I have been able to source quality Australian chestnut flour in many places on the internet. Chestnut flour adds sweetness and nuttiness to gluten free sourdough and it is also high in quality proteins, fibres, vitamins and minerals.

Water

Always use filtered, non-chlorinated, non-fluoridated water, especially for your starter culture. Chlorinated water will kill your wild-yeast starter/culture. I have a water filter attached to my kitchen tap, which makes obtaining filtered water very simple. Rainwater also makes a beautiful alternative—just make sure that you do not have any algae or dead animals in your rain water tank, as this will create mould in your starter. Do not use de-ionised ('dead') water (sold in supermarkets as distilled water).

TIPS **XANTHAM GUM SHOULD BE AVOIDED.**
It is used extensively in almost all commercially produced gluten-free bread flours as a replacement for the missing gluten. It is produced through a process involving fermentation of glucose or sucrose from corn by the Xanthomonas campestris bacterium. As most corn products are contaminated with genetically modified corn, so is xantham gum. Products containing xantham gum are best avoided for consumption by children as it causes constipation by absorbing water out of the body. There are many ways to mimic gluten in gluten-free bread without resorting to xantham gum. You will find out all about this in my gluten-free sourdough recipes.

Salt

Salt enhances the flavour of the bread. Sea-salt, lake salt, macrobiotic salt, fleur de sel or Celtic salt, ground or dissolved first, result in the best-tasting breads. Do not use salt with added 'free-flowing agent' (aluminum-based) and iodine. My preference is about 20 grams per kilo of flour (2 per cent). You may like to add less—say 10 grams per kilo of flour—it's up to your own taste.

It is important to add salt because:
- Salt controls your dough's fermentation, allowing you to have a long fermentation period.
- Salt increases the strength of the gluten by tightening the gluten structure. A salt-less dough will be slack and sticky and the bread volume will be poor.
- Salt enhances the colour of your crumb and increases its moistness.

> TIPS It is very important to remember that wet dough makes moist bread, so do not go overboard by adding more flour during kneading. If your dough still feels wet after some kneading, never add more flour without a mandatory rest of 20–30 minutes to allow the flour to absorb the water, especially for wholemeal flours.

A Note on Measurements

1 teaspoon = 5g
1 tablespoon = 15g (½oz)
Liquid measures
¼ teaspoon = 2.5ml
½ teaspoon = 2.5ml
1 teaspoon = 5ml
1 tablespoon = 20ml (Australian)

(Note: Imperial and NZ tablespoon is 15ml)

Solid measures (vary, depending on substance): 1 cup sunflower seeds=200g (6 ½oz)

Oven Temperatures

100°C = 200°F = Gas Mark 1
120°C = 250°F = Gas Mark 1
150°C = 300°F= Gas Mark 2
160°C = 325°F = Gas Mark 2–3
180°C = 350°F = Gas Mark 4
190°C = 375°F = Gas Mark 5
200°C = 400°F = Gas Mark 6
220°C = 420°F = Gas Mark 7
230°C = 450°F = Gas Mark 8
250°C = 485°F = Gas Mark 9

Sourdough Hot Cross Buns

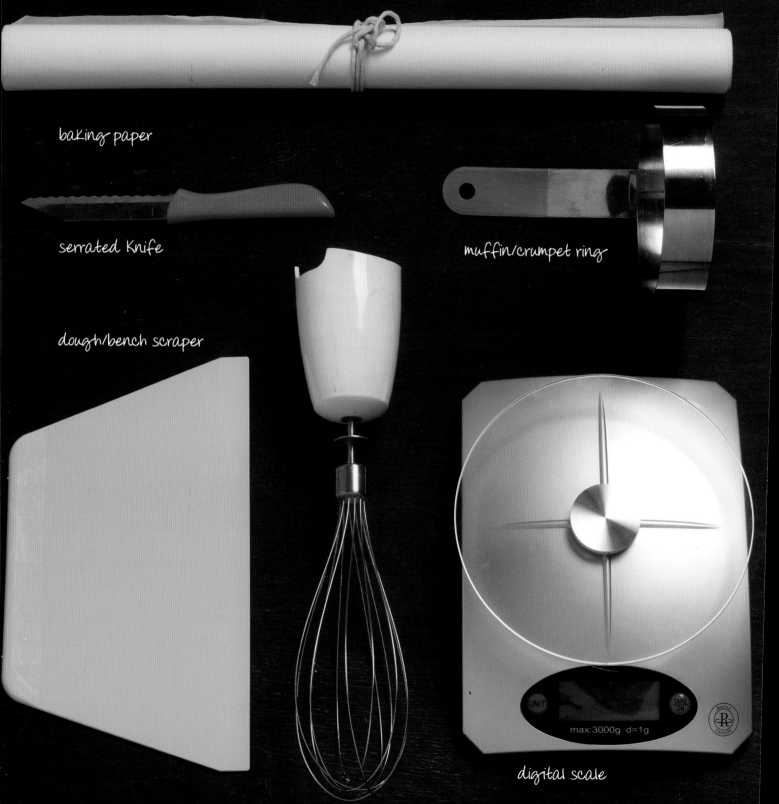

baking paper

serrated knife

muffin/crumpet ring

dough/bench scraper

digital scale

max:3000g d=1g

UNIT

TARE
ON

EQUIPMENT

Baking Equipment Essentials

The most essential piece of equipment you will ever need to make good sourdough bread is your hands. When I teach my sourdough bread classes, I teach people how to make bread by hand. Once you have made dough several times, you will always remember how this dough feels and you will be able to make perfect sourdough every time.

Only when you have mastered making sourdough bread by hand should you move on to dough-making machines such as breadmakers, or rotary machines such as Kitchen Aid or Kenwood Chef. Later in this chapter, the use of breadmakers and rotary mixers will be explained.

I understand if you prefer to use a machine and, if so, you can convert any of my recipes by replacing the mixing/resting/kneading part with your dough-making machine. You may also prefer to use your machine when working with a very wet dough, which is almost impossible to knead by hand.

I am a very practical cook—my focus is to get you inspired enough to make these sourdough breads, by whatever means (hands or machine) you prefer. It is entirely your choice as long as you get the result you wish for.

For my gluten-free batter, I prefer an electric or manual whisk. This tool mixes the batter well and creates a lovely 'airy', spongy consistency. A whisk allows you to incorporate an incredible amount of air—much more than a conventional mixer. This is important for making gluten-free bread, as you want the texture to be as light as possible—we do not want to create a dense cake.

NON-METALLIC CONTAINERS AND BOWLS

Due to the acidity of the sourdough and the length of the sourdough fermentation, it is important to use a non-metallic container or bowl for both your starter and dough. Any glass, ceramic or even a BPA-free plastic bowl is fine to use.

You also need a pop-able lid, so when the carbon-dioxide gas is expelled during fermentation, your glass container will not explode and break. Do not use a screw-top lid or airtight preserving jar—if it is glass, you will end up with a massive explosion in your kitchen.

The pH of a sourdough starter is about three or four. This is very acidic and it will react with any metal utensils, unless you have very good quality stainless steel.

DIGITAL OR ELECTRONIC SCALES

I believe that making bread is more of an art than a science. It is about building your intuition rather than mastering precision. You need to diligently measure your ingredients precisely so your own dough or starter will be as close as possible to what is required.

I weigh everything, apart from small amounts of spices, so I recommend that all ingredients, including water, are measured in grams and ounces using a digital scale. I use the metric system because of the global variability of volume measurements, such as cups or tablespoons/teaspoons: 500 grams (17oz) is the same anywhere in the world.

The best electronic scale is one that is calibrated to 1 or 2 grams and with a capacity of 5 or 10 kilos. Your bowl could already weigh 1–2 kilograms before you add any of the ingredients.

GRANITE TILE

Buying a piece of 10 millimetre-thick (0.4in) natural granite stone tile will be the best investment you are ever going to make for your sourdough bread-making. In my opinion, granite is a far superior heat conductor than any pizza stones or terracotta tiles. A thicker granite tile of 20 millimetres will not be effective at all because it will take hours to bring it to a useable temperature for your baking.

Always pre-heat your granite at least 30–45 minutes before baking. This pre-heated granite will give your bread dough a burst of searing heat, like a wood-fire oven floor, creating an instant oven spring (expansion) and a well-crusted bottom. Radiating heat from the granite tile will also cook your loaf more evenly and thoroughly. This high, searing heat is responsible for creating a brown crusty crust and large holes in the crumb and is especially important if you want a wood-fired 'artisan bread' look with a mouthwatering brown crusty crust and a soft interior crumb.

You can cheaply and easily find a piece of granite tile from your local tile shop. Make sure that your granite is cut from real granite, not composite granite. Composite granite is made from broken up pieces of granite and polymer resin, which is highly poisonous when baked, especially at the high baking temperatures used in these recipes.

DOUGH/BENCH SCRAPER

The incredibly cheap, plastic dough/bench scrapers are another vital and extremely useful tool in your bread-making process. They are very useful in kneading and moving wet dough, cutting your dough and are efficient for cleaning your bench, because they will not scratch the surface.

I like to have two of different sizes. For example, a small one measuring about 8.5 x 12cm (3.3 x 4.7in) with a curved edge, and a bigger one 12 x 21cm (4.7 x 8.2in) (see picture). I do not recommend metal scrapers as they will scratch your working surface, unless you have a stainless steel working surface. A kitchenware supply shop will stock these dough scrapers.

GARDEN/CLEANING MISTER

Another very useful tool that is readily available and very cheap is a liquid mister/spray bottle. This will moisten the surface of your dough and create a moist environment during baking to give you a crusty crust and an open crumb. Always fill the mister with clean filtered water and do not use your mister for any other purpose to avoid contamination/poisoning. You will find a liquid mister at your gardening shop or most supermarkets.

BAKER'S PIZZA PEEL

For those of you who prefer free-form loaves, I would recommend you buy a sturdy baker's peel or paddle, which are found in most good kitchen shops. I find the aluminium ones with long handles better for handling dough and easier to clean than the wooden paddles.

A baker's peel allows you to transport well-proofed dough to and from your bench to the hot granite surface in your oven, with ease and without burning your precious arms or hands.

BAKING/PARCHMENT PAPER

Baking/parchment paper is a piece of paper that has been surfaced with silicon. It is non-toxic because silicon is one of the most inert substances known to man. Baking paper is easily available at most grocery stores or supermarkets. Always choose the sturdiest, thickest premium baking paper. Do not skimp on this or you will be very sorry when your loaf is stuck onto the paper!

A real artisan baker uses a floured baker's peel to transport dough to and from the hot oven. However, you may find, as I have, that this is not an easy skill to master. Most likely, the dough will end up stuck onto the baker's peel or on the floor.

To overcome this problem, I have taught my students to put the shaped dough onto a piece of baking/parchment paper. This way, transporting the well-formed dough on or off the baker's peel and onto the hot granite surface can be done effortlessly. The baking paper can then be removed from the bread loaf about 15 minutes after baking and can be reused again and again.

TIPS   Another very helpful use of baking paper is to cover your rising dough before you put your wet towel over it. This will save you from baking your kitchen towel in the oven because your dough has stuck to it. If your dough is stuck onto your baking paper, you can still bake your dough because you can peel it off easily without taking any part of the stuck dough with it. Your loaf crust will remain perfect. Baking your kitchen towel with your loaf may sound hilarious but I will be the first to admit that this had happened to me over the years, more than once!

BAKING TINS

My students often ask me why I use baking tins when you can make free-form loaves. One reason for using tins is for making bread for sandwiches. Also free-form loaves have more crust than crumb, and my 12-year-old daughter will not eat the crust, therefore wasting most of the bread.

Another practical reason for using baking tins is, for first-time bakers, it is very easy to gauge whether the dough has doubled or not by judging how far your dough has risen in the tin.

(Believe me, baking the very first few loaves in tins has saved the wits of many of my first-time student bakers.)

Lastly, by using baking tins, you have the ability to rise and bake your bread at your convenience because it can happily rest in the fridge covered with wet cling wrap or inside a large, inflated plastic bag for a few hours or a couple of days.

The best baking tins are the commercial baking tins made from heavy-gauge aluminised steel alloy and enamelled with silicon. This baking tin requires no oiling or washing because nothing will stick to it and will last you almost half a lifetime if you look after it.

A wipe with a damp soft cloth is all the cleaning it needs after use. The heavy-gauge steel ensures efficient heat absorption and distribution, therefore the sides will brown before the top, ensuring an even cooking of the loaves and crusty brown crusts.

I only use two sizes of commercial baking tin (see picture):
- A small loaf tin: inner measurements are 10cm wide, 17cm long, and 10cm high (4 x 7.5 x 4in).
- A medium loaf tin: inner measurements are 10cm wide, 23.5cm long, and 10cm high (4 x 9.4 x 4in).

I do not recommend that you use any loaf tin larger than the medium-sized tin because your bread will not cook properly on the inside before the outside is burned. Under-cooked bread does not taste very nice and is indigestible.

COVERING THE DOUGH

The best way to keep your dough from drying out while it is rising is to use a container with a lid. If you do not have an enclosed container, another way to cover your dough is by using wet cling wrap because it will stick to almost anything.

Lay the cling wrap over the opening of your bowl, mist the surface of the cling wrap with your water mister, then flip the wrap swiftly over and onto the bowl. The water will ensure the cling wrap sticks to your bowl.

A wet tea towel is not a very good idea, for two reasons. In a dry continent, like Australia, your tea towel will become dry before your dough is completely risen. You also run the risk of your dough sticking to your tea towel. See the Tips on page 25.

Dried-out dough will hinder it from rising. It will form a very thick crust when baked and it will stop the crust from browning properly. Misting your dough at intervals as it is rising is therefore essential.

SERRATED KNIFE

Although you can buy fancy lamé knives to slash your loaves, a quality thin-blade, serrated knife does the job well—and it is safer for your fingers. I prefer a Victorinox vegetable peeler or steak knife as the thin blade keeps sharp for years. Most brands will have something similar to this thin-blade serrated knife.

medium tin

small tin

baguette tray

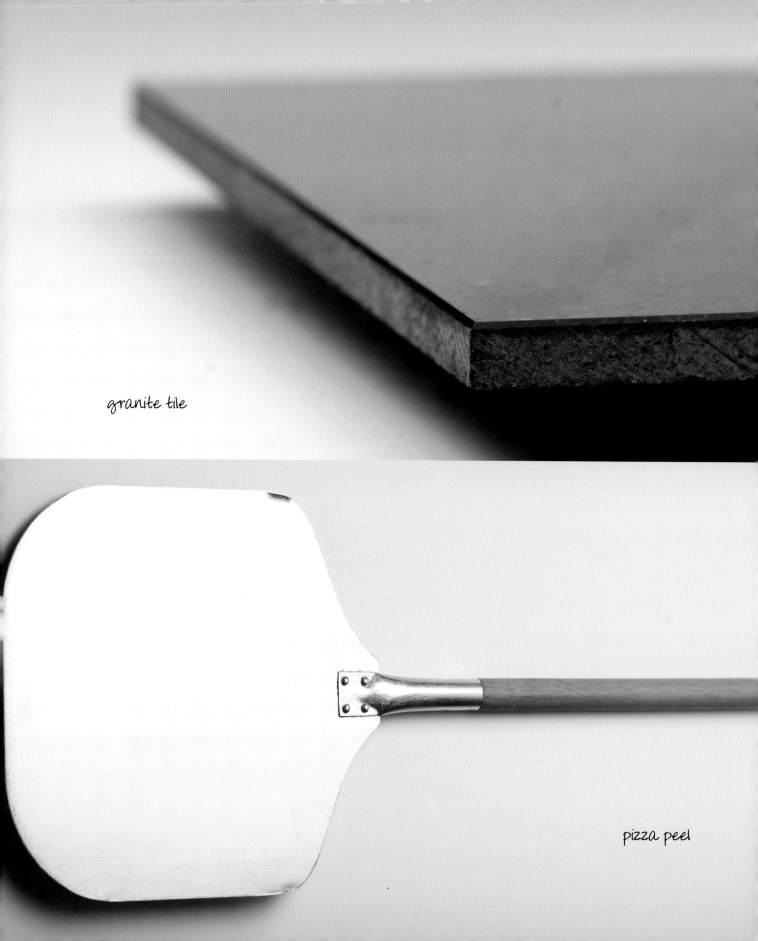

granite tile

pizza peel

ELECTRIC WHISK

For mixing gluten-free batter, an electric whisk is vital because it incorporates as much air as possible, giving you an airy, fluffy, luxurious batter resembling a thick mixture of beaten egg and sugar (like a sponge-cake mixture). You do not need to spend $100 or more for this, I have a very simple electric whisk that cost about $60, and it works brilliantly.

You can also use your electric whisk to mix your starter, for ease and comfort. Your starter will be very happy because of the abundance of 'oxygen' as the whisk aerates the starter batter, giving you a very spongy (rye) or bubbly (wheat or spelt) starter.

OVEN THERMOMETER

Every oven is different. I have two ovens of the same make and model, but each behaves differently. It is important that you make the time to get to know your oven intimately because this is crucial to the success of your bread.

Do yourself a big favour and buy an oven thermometer. This is a cheap but very useful tool to know the real temperature of your oven.

There will also be hot spots in your oven. To know where hot spots are, lay a piece of baking paper to cover a rack in the middle shelf of your oven and turn your oven on for about 10 minutes at 200°C (390°F). On the 'browned' baking paper, you will see a pattern of where your oven hot spots are. You will then know how and where to rotate your bread loaves during baking to get an evenly cooked loaf.

COOLING RACK

I use oven racks to cool my loaves. However, if yours do not suffice, make sure you have a cooling rack so that the freshly baked bread can cool down effectively, allowing air to circulate on the bottom and sides of the loaves. Bread continues to cook as it cools, so it is important to allow this cooling process to occur naturally before slicing your loaf.

Using machines

BREADMAKERS

I use a breadmaker solely to mix and knead the dough. Breadmakers, in my experience, do a better job at kneading dough than rotary mixers because they create less heat as they knead. However, you must ensure that the often built-in heating element does not kick in at the end of the kneading cycle for automatically rising the dough.

Due to the absence of overheating, compared to rotary mixers, your breadmaker will last longer and, at a fraction of the price of a good rotary mixer, is a far better option for kneading dough.

One feature I do not like is the teflon coating on the bread pan and the dough paddle(s) because teflon, when ingested, is poisonous. Make sure that the teflon surface remains intact on both the pan and the paddles. Replace immediately if it is peeling. Never ever use metal utensils inside your breadmaker pan.

I use the 23-minute 'pasta cycle' on my Sunbeam breadmaker as this allows sufficient time for mixing and kneading the dough without the heating element turning on. I pause the cycle after 5 minutes of mixing to rest the dough. This is an important step because this will allow the gluten in the dough to relax, a process called autolysis, and it allows time for the flour, especially wholemeal flour, to absorb the water.

I often turn off the cycle halfway as I feel that the dough has had sufficient kneading. Remember, over-kneading will heat up your dough, which in turn means oxidation of the flours, making your bread insipid and flavourless. It is really important that you do not take your eyes off the dough. The message here is to use your breadmaker as an extension of your hands, so you are still in control of the whole process.

SPIRAL AND PLANETARY MIXERS

The two most common types of mixer are spiral mixers and planetary mixers. A spiral mixer is a mixer where the bowl moves around a vertical axis and has a spinning spiral hook. It is superior to the planetary mixer because it does not heat up the dough, even though it kneads the dough faster than a planetary mixer. Most commercial mixers are spiral mixers. I have seen some smaller spiral mixers from Italy, which are worth searching for.

Planetary mixers have a moving head that moves around the stationary bowl. These are multifunctional mixers that can be used to do a variety of tasks, such as beating and mixing cakes. Most, if not all, domestic mixers are planetary mixers, including those made by Kitchen Aid and Kenwood Chef.

The downsides to these machines are that:
- they tend to heat up the dough very quickly.
- they can produce uneven mixing if the dough sticks onto the kneading hook.
- they can handle only a small amount of dough.
- the motor will overheat and wear out fast if you use it too frequently for kneading dough.

TIPS One way to overcome overheating is to use the machine as an extension of your hands, so you are still in control of the whole process. You need to stop/rest your machine frequently to reduce overheating. And always make sure that you do not overload the machine with too much dough. Remember, heating up your dough also means oxidation of the flours, rendering your bread insipid and flavourless. Follow your mixer manufacturer's instructions and never forget to use your intuitive experience for what the dough should feel like.

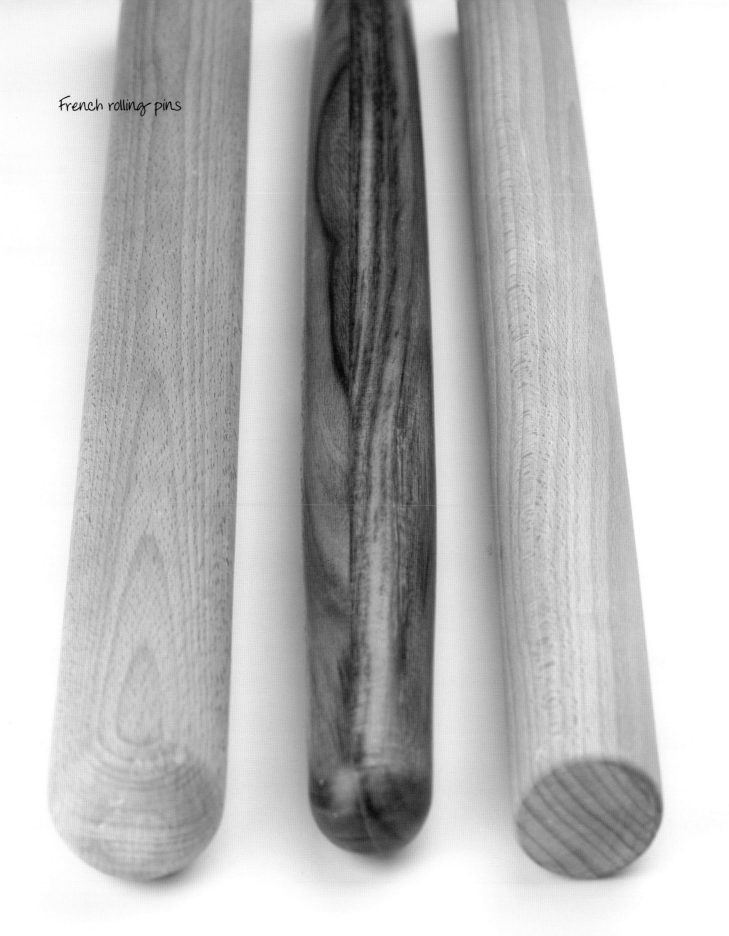

French rolling pins

active rye starter

ALL ABOUT
SOURDOUGH STARTER

Imagine this world without the magic of wild fermentation—we would not have wine, cheese, beer, pickles, yoghurt, miso, tempeh—and of course the most precious staff of life, bread. Humans have been obsessed with wild fermentation for thousands of years: it is merely the transformation of food products by bacteria (lactic bacteria) and yeast. Just about anything can be fermented: grapes, soya bean, milk, grains, flour and even meat and fish. During a controlled fermentation process, yeast and/or bacteria digest sugar and/or protein, to produce the desired end product. The byproducts of this process are carbon dioxide, alcohol and organic acids such as lactic acids and acetic acids.

Our ancestors have been fermenting flour and water to make sourdough bread for centuries. Even with the advent of modern, fast commercial bread making, slowly fermented sourdough breads still produce the more nourishing and more delicious bread for human consumption.

Commercial yeast, developed from a single strain of wild yeast, create a fast acting and robust leavening agent. Wild yeast and lactic bacteria in natural sourdough fermentation, on the other hand, are, without a doubt, the more temperamental and less predictable sisters. They require patience, persistence and careful attention. However, your effort will be rewarded with bread that has a deliciously complex flavour and is nutritionally better than commercial yeasted bread. Only the long and slow fermentation of sourdough yeasts and bacteria will coax and tease out the full flavour and nutrients of grains. This is because these delicious organic acids take about 8–12 hours to be produced by the lactic bacteria.

If you speed up the fermentation process of your sourdough bread making by introducing heat, your resulting sourdough will be devoid of the benefits of the lactobacterial fermentation, leaving you with an insipid flavoured bread that lacks the nutritional profile of naturally fermented sourdough bread. Unfortunately, in countries where the method of bread production is not strictly regulated (such as Australia), proofing at a higher temperature is common practice in commercial sourdough bread production, so that the heat-loving wild yeast flourishes and rises the bread fully before the lactobacteria have a chance to work into the dough.

To make sourdough bread, you must first understand and master the art, and maybe a little science, of creating, feeding and looking after your very own sourdough starter. You do not need to be discouraged by the common sourdough myth that the 100-year-old sourdough starter from Paris or San Francisco is somewhat superior to one made in any other part of the world. You also need not be worried that you will have to eat, sleep and rest with your sourdough starter 24 hours a day and that it will die of neglect if you do not feed it every day. None of this is true! Fortunately, you need nothing more than the best quality wholegrain/wholemeal flour and filtered water to start creating your very own starter.

One thing I need to mention to you, is that sourdough does not mean sour-tasting bread. In Italy and France, sour-tasting bread is regarded as a sign of negligence on the part of the bakers. Even in Germany, where the more acidic rye starter is widely used, the goal is not to create mouth-puckering bread. So it is important that at no time do you use a starter in your dough that smells and tastes like vinegar! We are not here to make sauerkraut.

If your starter smells too sour, you need to throw out most of it, leaving a couple of tablespoons or a quarter of a cup, and move the remainder to a new clean container and start again, by feeding it the right ratio of flour and water. Sour-, or worse still, foul-smelling starter is caused by over-fermenting or neglect from not using your starter for a while, or a combination of both. The more you use and feed your starter (at least once a week), the happier and better (bubblier) your starter will become. Any time your starter is not being used, it needs to live in the fridge.

So, what does a healthy starter smell, look and taste like? A healthy starter is characterised by a fruity, cider-smelling aroma; it has lots of bubbles and looks either frothy or spongy; and when you put a little starter on your tongue it will fizz and taste like fresh cider, a little tangy but not overly sour, and, most importantly, there is no smell of vinegar or alcohol!

Vinegar and alcohol, the by-products of the wild yeast and lactobacteria fermentation, both act as preservatives to your precious starter, so you do need to have some of these. Too much vinegar and alcohol, however, will eventually kill both the wild yeast and bacteria. Remember, we use alcohol and vinegar as sterilisation agents to kill any bacteria or viruses.

There are two forms of starter: liquid and stiff. I prefer a liquid starter as this is much easier and more practical to use for home sourdough bread making. A low temperature will produce a sourer starter, because lactobacteria prefer a lower temperature to ferment. Rye starter also produces a sourer starter. However, rye has more sugars than wheat or spelt so rye starter is more resistant to abuse and neglect. White starter, on the other hand, will start as a mild-tasting starter, but will go sour very quickly if you do not use it immediately after it is activated and bubbly.

The best temperature for sourdough is between 18–28°C (65–83°F) but a lower temperature just means it takes longer to ferment your starter or dough. A higher temperature means it will ferment faster. In most cases, a comfortable room temperature is fine. If you live in a very cold climate, you can grow your starter in an esky equipped with a hot water bottle or in the sink filled with warm water.

Create your very own starter culture

Levain or sourdough starter culture is simply created by mixing wholegrain/whole meal flour (preferably organic rye) with water. You are basically encouraging the wild yeast, normally occurring in the grains, to grow and create the fermentation.

STEP ONE ON DAY ONE:

- In a glass or plastic container, with a pop-up lid (not a screw-top lip), add 100g (3 ½oz) of wholemeal rye flour and 200g (7oz) of water to make a loose pancake batter. Stir or whisk well to incorporate as much oxygen as possible.
- With the lid closed, leave the starter to ferment in the warmest place in your house, 18-28°C (64-83°F).
- After about 12–48 hours, have a look at your starter. It should start to show some sign of bubbles. If there are not many bubbles at this stage, do not worry.

STEP TWO ON DAY TWO:

After your starter shows the first sign of bubbles:

- Throw out half of your starter.
- Add 50g (1 ¾oz) of rye flour and 100g (3 ½oz) of water. Stir or whisk well.
- With the lid closed, leave the starter to ferment in the warmest place in your house, 18-28°C (64-83°F).
- This mixture will thin out as it is fermenting and becoming bubbly.
- After about 6–12 hours, have a look at your starter. It should have some more bubbles and look either foamy or spongy, depending on how 'wholegrain' your wholemeal rye flour is.

For another one to three days, repeat step two above, until your starter is full of foamy/frothy bubbles or has the consistency of a spongy mousse.

- You can now add 100g (3 ½oz) rye flour and 150g (5oz) water, whisk/mix well, then leave for 6–12 hours to ferment.
- Once your starter is risen and full of bubbles or spongy, your rye starter is ready for use!

Create a white or wholemeal wheat or spelt starter

Luckily for all sourdough enthusiasts, we do not need to keep several types of starters. We only need to keep one healthy starter, namely, a wholemeal rye starter. If you need a white or wholemeal wheat or spelt starter, you need to:

- Use 1-2 tablespoons of your live rye starter and mix with your desired flour and water. The ratio for wheat and spelt is different to rye, the ratio is one part flour to one part water in grams or ounces (for example if you use 100g (3 ½oz) of flour, then you need 100g (3 ½oz) water).
- Keep in a warm place until active (6–12 hours).
- Wheat or spelt starter becomes over-fermented very quickly and turns vinegary and sour. My advice is to always make just enough for what you need and throw away what is left over, unless you want to use it again in a day or two.
- Wheat or spelt starter is hard to keep as it becomes very active (over-ferments) quickly and is easily contaminated, if not used daily or every couple of days.

Sourdough starter maintenance: looking after and using your starter

1. HOW TO FEED/ACTIVATE YOUR SOURDOUGH STARTER

6–12 hours before you want to make the sourdough e.g. the night or morning before you want to make bread:

- Take your starter out of the fridge, let it thaw out for a couple of hours.
- Add organic whole rye flour and water, in the ratio of 1:1.5 (e.g. 100g (3 ½oz) flour to 150g (5oz) water is a good quantity).
- Stir/whisk vigorously to add oxygen into the starter mixture.
- Keep starter in a warm place, but not in front of direct heat.
- Within 6–12 hours your starter will be bubbly and active.

Once your starter is active, you can use it in the next 12–24 hours.

If you are having problem with a sluggish/overly sour/separated starter:

- Throw out all but a quarter of a cup of starter, feed with 75g (2 ½oz) of rye flour and 150g (5oz) of water.
- Add extra water to your starter. Also, keeping your starter in a warmer place will help invigorate a sluggish starter.

In cold weather, you can put your container of starter in a sink full of warm water or in a warm (no more than 35°C/95°F) oven or dehydrator.

2. HOW TO LOOK AFTER YOUR STARTER IN-BETWEEN USE:

- Immediately after you have taken away the starter you need for your dough, add organic whole rye flour and water, in the ratio of 1:1.5. Use a smaller amount of flour (e.g. 50g (1 ¾oz) flour to 75g (2 ½oz) water.
- Stir vigorously to add oxygen into the starter mixture.
- Straight away put your starter, with a closed lid, in the fridge until you want to activate it.
- It will be fine in the fridge for about two weeks.

3. IF YOU ARE GOING AWAY FOR MORE THAN A MONTH YOU CAN EITHER:

1. Dry your active starter
- Spread your active starter thinly on baking paper, using a flat spatula
- Dry on the kitchen bench or outside under the sun or in a 35-37°C (95°F) dehydrator.
- DO NOT DRY IN THE OVEN.
- Dry starter has an infinite lifespan. Keep it in a double enclosed paper bag in a dark, cool place.
- Before use, pulverise your starter (about 50-75g/1 ¾-2 ½oz) into powder using a coffee grinder or food processor, then add 100g (3 ½oz) organic whole rye flour and 150g (5oz) warm water.
- Keep in a warm place until active and bubbly, about 12 hours.

OR

2. Make a solid starter (often referred to as desem):
- Mix your active starter with as much rye flour to make a solid ball of dough. Kept adding rye flour until you can roll your 'starter' dough into a ball.
- Wrap in baking paper and put inside a zip-locked bag or an airtight container. Put in the fridge until you are ready to use it.
- When you are ready, pinch about 25–50g (¾–1 ¾oz) of this solid starter/desem.
- Using your fingertips break apart the desem and then add 150g (5oz) warm water, and continue to dissolve the desem into the water.
- Slowly add 150g (5oz) of rye flour into the mixture and mix well until the starter mixture is homogenous.
- Cover with a lid and leave to ferment in a warm place.

TIPS: After use, in between use, or if you are confused and don't know what to do with your starter—KEEP YOUR STARTER IN THE FRIDGE. Refrigeration will slow down the rate of activity (fermentation) of the bacteria and yeast, so it will not over-ferment.

Things to remember

1. Your starter is the power engine of your sourdough bread. If your dough fails to rise the first time, the most likely cause is a sluggish or inactive starter.

2. Your starter will be in prime condition if you use it once a week. If you do not use it regularly, it will start to accumulate organic acids (vinegar, lactic acids) and alcohol. In small amounts, the organic acids are necessary to keep the starter from other harmful bacteria, but in larger amounts, these organic acids will send your starter to a slow, painful death.

3. To avoid unpleasant-tasting bread, keep your starter quantity at a minimum; throw away excess starter after you finish using it or before you start feeding for use. Allow no more than a quarter or half a cup of starter as your starting point before feeding (about 50-100g/1 ¾–3½oz).

4. Do not feed your starter with premix bread flours, as these premixes often contain commercial yeast, preservatives, emulsifiers—additives that will kill your sourdough starter's wild yeasts and lactobacilli in a matter of days.

5. The sourdough starter culture naturally creates its own by-products of vinegar and alcohol. If you have left your fermented starter for too long this vinegar and alcohol separate from the starter and form a layer of greyish liquid. To save your starter, you need to:
- throw out this liquid and the top two-thirds of the starter, before feeding. Rescue about a quarter of a cup or a couple of tablespoon of starter at the bottom of your container
- You need only a tablespoon of your old starter to start a new batch.
- Using a new clean container, start a new starter by feeding your remaining 1-2 tablespoons or ¼ cup of starter with 100g (3 ½oz) rye flour and 150g (5oz) water.

6. If your starter continually goes mouldy or becomes slimy with a foul smell, the most likely cause is that your water or flour could be contaminated with mould or algae. Another possibility is you have mould growing near where you store your starter. Clean your container and fridge with vinegar to get rid of mould. Throw away your flour and water, start with a new pack of flour and a new water source.

7. If all else fails, I have recently made my own wild sourdough starter (both rye starter and gluten-free starters) available for purchase from my website www.wildsourdough.com.au.

dried starter

active white starter

Characteristics of active/ripe starters

Size increase
All starter will have increased in size as it is fermenting. Some can double in size as the wild yeast multiply and carbon dioxide gas is produced. Once risen, this starter will collapse, as is the nature of the beast! You will see the evidence of this by the amount of starter creeping on the side of your container. This is the best time to use your starter as the organisms are hungry for a feed.

Abundance of bubbles
A ripe starter will be full of bubbles. This web of bubbles will range from gelatinous bubbles for white starter to spongy or mousse-like network of bubbles for stoneground wholemeal rye starter. Thinner starter will be gelatinous in consistency almost like a melting ice cream. This is often the case with wheat or spelt starters and is caused by the presence of gluten forming proteins.

Aroma
The aroma of a ripe starter is like cider—fresh, fruity, earthy, a little 'sour smell' but never overwhelmingly strong. It should smell fresh and must never smell strongly of vinegar or alcohol. If it does smell of vinegar or alcohol, your starter has over-fermented and your resulting bread will be unpleasantly sour and may not rise well. Remember, alcohol and vinegar will not rise any bread!

Taste
I know most of you will be reluctant to taste your starter, but I can assure you it does not taste bad. A ripe starter taste like a fizzy yoghurt, milky sweet with a detectable fizziness when it hits your tongue.

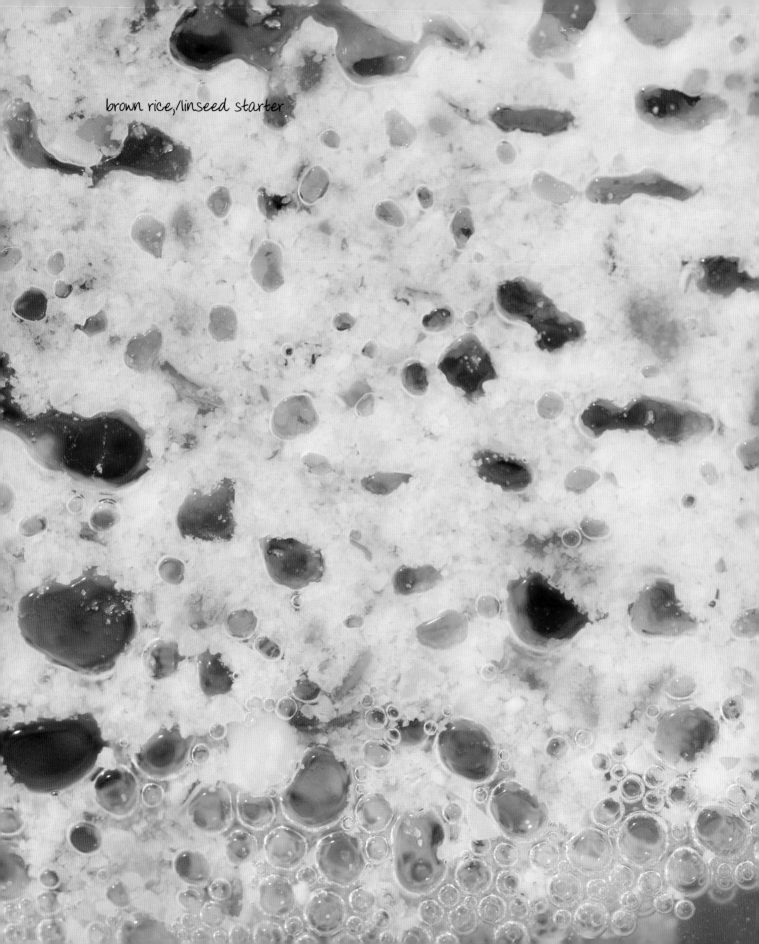
brown rice,/linseed starter

GLUTEN-FREE BREAD MAKING AND STARTER

This chapter is dedicated to those suffering from coeliac disease who are willing to go 'the whole nine yards' in search of the best tasting and nourishing bread, free from yeast and unnecessary additives (such as possibly-genetically modified infected xantham gums, emulsifier, soya, corn etc). Read also 'The History of Wheat and Coeliac Disease'.

Unless we resort to artificial gluten replacements (e.g. xantham gum), loads of yeast and nutritionally devoid starches, we will have problems trying to emulate 'real bread'. We cannot (nor do we want to) make 'fluffy white commercial bread' with real sourdough, without the addition of yeast and additives. I pride myself on being a cook/baker making food from wholesome natural ingredients, not an industrial chemist making 'fake' food.

So, with this in mind, let us make a new generation of bread, in a class of its own—wholegrain sourdough gluten-free bread. I have aimed for a sourdough bread that has good texture (easy to cut, not cakey or crumbly), good taste and is good for you.

Being a practical cook, I have devised a method that is manageable for most of you in your home kitchen, without causing you too much stress and bother. I wanted to create breads that are made from ingredients that are nutritious (as much wholegrain as possible), and easy to find in your local shops, at reasonable cost. I have avoided using soya and corn, as many people have become allergic to these two most common flours, used in disguise in many food products such as ice-cream, chewing gum, mayonnaise and more.

In order to do this, I have spent a lot of time experimenting and thinking—there have been lots of trials, errors and countless failures. Finally, a breakthrough happened, and I began to understand the sense and sensibility of gluten-free sourdough. This is what I want to share with you, my understanding and principles of gluten-free sourdough.

DOUGH VERSUS BATTER
- Forget all you have learned about making sourdough-like dough, we are not making dough here—in gluten-free sourdough we will be making a cake batter. It is paramount that you understand the right consistency of the batter.

RATIO OF STARTER TO FLOUR
- In sourdough breadmaking, we use a smaller amount of starter to the total flour used, e.g. 15-30 per cent of starter to flour
- In gluten-free sourdough we will be using more starter to flour, e.g. 65-75 per cent starter to flour. We are basically mixing a small amount of flour to a large quantity of starter.

MIXING/WHISKING

- You need to whisk your gluten-free batter at least twice, with a half an hour rising time, in between. This will give your gluten-free loaf a finer 'crumb'.
- I prefer an electric whisk for speed and strength. However, a hand whisker will do just fine.

USE OF TINS

- Gluten-free dough is a liquid batter, therefore, gluten-free loaves can only be baked in a tin, as it needs a container to hold itself up. You can make muffins or pancakes using a muffin/tins or egg rings.
- There is no 'dough' that can be shaped into a free-form loaf.

RISING AND BAKING

- Your sourdough gluten-free batter should rise only once, not twice.
- Unlike normal sourdough or yeasted bread, where you bake the loaf when it is completely risen (at its peak) for your gluten-free loaf, you put into the oven when it is slightly under-risen. This way your loaf will rise and give you a flat or, if you are lucky, a dome-shaped crust instead of a sunken top. If you bake your gluten-free loaf when it is fully risen, it will deflate as soon as you move the tin, giving you a very dense loaf with a sunken crust.
- Baking gluten-free sourdough is always done at a much lower temperature (200ºC/400ºF to 180ºC/350ºF) for over an hour, because it is a batter not a dough. You need to cook and dry out the crumb without burning the crust.
- Your loaf will lose a lot of water during its baking, about 10–15 per cent is common.
- Testing with a skewer is difficult, because in most cases, the crumb will remain moist.
- There is nothing worse than uncooked gluten-free bread because the crumb is so moist. If you are unsure whether your bread is cooked or not, it is best to cook it for another 20–30 minutes longer. This will do no harm!
- All gluten-free sourdough bread has a moist crumb, and it is denser than my wheat/spelt sourdough. However, you can achieve a lighter, spongier texture by using mostly buckwheat flour, rather than rice flour.

CUTTING AND FREEZING

- Do not cut your gluten-free sourdough loaf while it is warm—wait until it is completely cool.
- Gluten-free loaf is best sliced, then frozen. As this is a very dense loaf, it will take a long time to thaw out a whole loaf. Frozen slices can be easily toasted with or without thawing.

KEEPING STARTER

- Gluten-free starter must be kept in the fridge at all times, unless you are activating it for use. It is more fragile than rye starter and will go off very easily if kept at room temperature for too long.

- Activate gluten-free starter anytime using water kefir, kefir milk or a teaspoon of active rye starter.

COMMON PROBLEMS

These are the common problems of gluten-free bread:

- hole in the middle—an uncooked crumb will create a hole in the middle of the loaf.
- crumb too moist and heavy—too much water needs light flour such as potato or tapioca.
- crumb too moist—under-cooked, needs to be cooked more.

Gluten-free starters

I have to limit myself to making only two major types of gluten-free starter at home, one is a brown rice starter and the other is a buckwheat starter. Why? Brown rice and buckwheat are very easy to ferment and both these flours are readily available at reasonable cost. You can also add one more—a sorghum starter or a buckwheat/sorghum starter. Sorghum, however, is not an easy flour to find.

I also add either (or both) chia seeds and linseeds to my brown rice starter, to add body and to eliminate the problem of the starter separating. Chia and linseed acts as a glue to keep the consistency of the brown rice starter whole, not separating into liquid and solid.

You can start a gluten-free sourdough starter the same way you start a rye or wheat sourdough starter (see 'All about sourdough starter'). However, you can jump-start this process by using a teaspoon of your active rye starter to a mixture of brown rice/buckwheat flour and water, let it ferment and bubble, throw away most of it, feed again with more water and flour, and do this two or three more times to get rid of most of the rye flour in your initial starter. You will end up with a gluten-free starter eventually.

For those kefir aficionados, you can add a tablespoon or two of your active fermented kefir milk or, better still, water kefir. Kefir, like sourdough, has both wild yeast and lactobacillus. Therefore, it is perfect for jump-starting your gluten-free sourdough starter. The starter will start to ferment and bubble immediately within 6–12 hours.

Like sourdough, kefir grains are a combination of bacteria and yeasts living symbiotically in a medium (most common medium is milk) that contains proteins, lipids, and sugars. This symbiotic bacteria and yeast form 'kefir grains' that resemble tiny cauliflowers. Yeast and bacteria convert proteins, lipids and sugar into a nourishing fermented tonic rich in vitamin B, folic acids and, of course, alive probiotics. There are two different types of kefir; milk kefir and water kefir. Milk kefir is grown in milk and water kefir lives in sugary water. I feed my water kefir with dried figs, fruit and a squeeze of lemon juice or coconut water (not coconut milk). Note: There is a small amount of alcohol (2-3 per cent) being produced during fermentation, so do not drink kefir and drive!

Unlike wheat/spelt/rye starter, which starts as a thick starter and thins out to a bubbly pancake batter after fermentation, gluten-free starter will start as a thin mixture, then it will swell and become a thick spongy mixture. Pure brown rice starter will separate, like whey and curd, but the underneath 'curd' part is thick and spongy.

To be practical, as most of us have a limited space in our fridge, it is best to keep the minimum number of starters. The three types of gluten-free starter I use are:

1. BUCKWHEAT STARTER

I love both the texture and taste of buckwheat sourdough breads. Also, buckwheat starter does not separate. It rises so readily and gives you the most spongy, silky starter, almost like the texture of melting ice-cream.

2. BUCKWHEAT/SORGHUM STARTER

This starter is created for those of you who do not like the taste and smell of buckwheat. I have diluted the strong taste of buckwheat with sorghum—sorghum gives sponginess to the starter/bread, but it also has a neutral taste and smell. You still need the buckwheat flour for its silky and gelatinous texture. In your final dough, you can add ground caraway or fennel seeds to give the buckwheat bread a beautiful mellowed complex aroma and, of course, some sweetener to get rid of the bitterness.

3. BROWN RICE/LINSEED STARTER

I have added linseed to my basic brown rice starter because I wanted to create a starter that does not separate. Brown rice starter will separate immediately after you mix it, which can be very discouraging. Linseed adds body and 'glues' the mixture together to create a thick spongy starter. It is highly indigestible unless it is soaked or fermented for a long period of time, so the more time fermenting it, the better.

You can keep two starters—buckwheat and brown rice/linseed starter—then just add some sorghum into your buckwheat starter, should you wish to have a buckwheat/sorghum starter.

TIPS: Making the starter, making the batter, and rising the batter for gluten-free sourdough bread is very easy but the fate of your sourdough loaf is in the baking.

Remember, we need to cook bread by drying the crumb, so low temperature and long baking time are critical to the success of your gluten-free sourdough baking.

buckwheat starter

Creating a gluten-free buckwheat starter

Buckwheat starter will start off thin, but will thicken, rise and swell up during fermentation.

DAY 1:
- Put a tablespoon of sourdough rye starter, or a tablespoon of water kefir or milk kefir, in a glass or plastic container with a pop-up lid (not a screw-top lip).
- Add 100g (3 ½oz) of buckwheat flour and 200g (7oz) of filtered water, stir or whisk well.
- With the lid closed, leave the starter to ferment in the warmest place in your house (18-28°C/65-83°F)
- This mixture is thin to start off with.
- After about 6–12 hours, have a look at your starter—it will have risen. The texture will be spongy and very thick.
- Leave in fridge overnight.

DAY 2:
- Throw out half of your starter.
- Add 50g (1 ¾oz) of buckwheat flour and 100g (3 ½oz) of filtered water, stir or whisk well
- With the lid closed, leave the starter to ferment in the warmest place in your house (18–28°C/65-83°F).
- This mixture is thin to start off with.
- After about 6–12 hours, have a look at your starter, it would have risen and it will be spongy and very thick.
- Leave in fridge overnight.

DAY 3 (6-12 HOURS BEFORE YOU WANT TO USE YOUR STARTER):
- Throw out half of your starter.
- Add 200g (7oz) of buckwheat flour and 400g (14oz) of filtered water: stir or whisk well. The mixture will look runny at this time, do not worry.
- With the lid closed, leave the starter to ferment in the warmest place in your house (18–28°C/65-83°F).
- After about 6–12 hours, this starter will thicken, rise and swell into a thick mousse. Your starter is now ready for use!

TIPS BUCKWHEAT FEEDING RATIO (IN WEIGHT)—1 BUCKWHEAT FLOUR : 2 WATER
e.g. A common feeding ratio for one loaf is 200g (7oz) buckwheat flour, 400g (14oz) water (e.g. 2 x 200g). This will give you a total starter of 600g (21oz), plus whatever initial quantity of starter you have in your container.

Gluten-free buckwheat/sorghum starter

Once you have your buckwheat starter active and ready, you can create a new starter by adding sorghum flour and water.

6-12 HOURS BEFORE YOU WANT TO USE YOUR STARTER:
- Take your buckwheat starter out of the fridge.
- Add 100g (3 ½oz) of buckwheat flour, 100g (3 ½oz) sorghum flour and 400g (14oz) of filtered water. Stir or whisk well. The mixture will look runny at this time.
- With the lid closed, leave the starter to ferment in the warmest place in your house (18–28°C/65–83°F).
- After about 6–12 hours, this starter will thicken, rise and swell into a thick batter. Your starter is now ready for use!

> TIPS BUCKWHEAT/SORGHUM FEEDING RATIO (IN WEIGHT)—1 BUCKWHEAT FLOUR: 1 SORGHUM FLOUR: 4 WATER
> eg. A common feeding ratio for one loaf: 100g (3 ½oz) buckwheat flour, 100g (3 ½oz) sorghum, 4 x 100g water (400g/14oz). This will give you a total starter of 600g (21oz), plus whatever leftover starter is in your container.

Gluten-free brown rice/linseed starter

Brown rice/linseed starter will start off as a thin watery starter, which will separate during fermentation. After you mix the two separate layers of water and thick batter, the resulting starter mixture will be quite thick.

DAY 1:
- In a glass or plastic container, with a pop-up lid (not a screw top lip), start with a tablespoon of sourdough buckwheat or rye starter or a tablespoon of water kefir or milk kefir.
- Add 100g (3 ½oz) of brown rice flour and 125g (4oz) of filtered water, stir or whisk well.
- With the lid closed, leave starter to ferment in the warmest place in your house (18-28°C/64-82°F).
- This mixture will separate into two layers, with a layer of water on top and a thick batter underneath.
- After about 6-8 hours, the bottom layer will be spongy. Leave in fridge overnight.

DAY 2:
- Throw out half of your starter.
- Add 50g (1 ¾oz) of brown rice flour and 75g (2 ½oz) of filtered water, stir or whisk well.
- With the lid closed, leave starter to ferment in the warmest place in your house (18-28°C/64-82°F).
- This mixture will separate into two layers, with a layer of water on top and a thick batter underneath.
- After about 6-8 hours, the bottom layer will be spongy. Leave in fridge until you are ready the next day.

DAY 3 OR 6-12 HOURS YOU WANT TO USE YOUR STARTER:
- Throw out half of your starter.
- Add 150g (5oz) of brown rice flour, 50g (1 ¾oz) of ground linseed (linseed meal) and 325g (11oz) of water, stir or whisk well. The mixture will look runny.
- With the lid closed, leave starter to ferment in the warmest place in your house (18–28°C/65–83°F).
- After about 6–8 hours, this mixture will not have separated and, instead, would have thickened into a thick spongy batter. Your starter is now ready for use!

TIPS: BROWN RICE/LINSEED FEEDING RATIO (IN WEIGHT)—1 GROUND LINSEED: 3 BROWN RICE: 6.5 WATER

e.g. A common feeding ratio for one loaf: 60g (2oz) ground linseed, 3x60g brown rice (180g/6oz), 6.5x75g water (390g/13 ¾ oz). This will give you a total starter of 630g (22oz), plus whatever leftover starter is in your container.

rising free-form loaves

SOURDOUGH BREAD MAKING STEP-BY-STEP

Here I will explain my most common sourdough bread making method in my basic recipes. You will find that my method will be different from other author's or baker's methods. Once you have mastered this method you will be able to understand and apply yourself to any of the recipes in the book. Each recipe is different with slight variations in time or order of steps for each recipe, so please follow the direction on each recipe precisely. Remember, using the same ingredients, a different method will produce a different loaf of bread, so you need to pay attention to each recipe.

All recipes in this book require the use of an active starter, so you must start the day/night before (6–12 hours before) you wish to make your bread. For instruction regarding activating your starter, please refer to the 'All about Sourdough Starter' chapter in this book. Note that each recipe calls for a different type of starter, so you need to use the starter prescribed in each recipe, or your resulting sourdough loaf will not be the same as the recipe intended.

1. Measure ingredients

I prefer to use a digital scale to weigh all ingredients, including the water. You need to be precise to create the right consistency for the dough. All the measurements in my recipes are in grams/ounces because any volume measuring apparatus can differ from country to country (eg. US cup measurement is 200ml, Australian cup measurement is 250ml) and measurement by volume for flours/dry ingredients is highly inaccurate. For practicality, some small quantity ingredients such as spices, salt etc are measured in teaspoon/tablespoons to make it more practical for you.

Make a habit of measuring your ingredients in this logical order of liquid first (starter, water, milk etc), then flours and lastly salt. If you do it this way, you do not need to panic if you make a mistake e.g. if you add too much flour or salt, you can take away flour or salt, easily.

Make sure you use non-chlorinated/non-fluoridated water and pure sea salt or lake salt (see chapter on ingredients). You also need to measure correctly the ratio of flour to water in the starter recipe. The little effort of being accurate will go a long way, especially for novice bakers.

2. Mix ingredients

Once you have weighed all ingredients into your bowl, you can start to stir and mix ingredients together using a strong (steel reinforced) silicone spatula or a wooden spoon, until they form a cohesive mass. The dough mixture will start off as quite dry but as you mix and stir, the water will be slowly absorbed into the flour and the dough mixture will become the right consistency.

Do not panic and start adding water to the mixture!

After about 5 minutes of continuous mixing, the dough will be moist/slightly wet and you can stop mixing once the dough is homogeneous with no visible bits of flour anywhere. If this is not the case, then you need to add some water to correct the consistency. This may be necessary if your flour has a higher gluten or humidity content than my local flour.

The more thorough your mixing is, the less kneading is required. Once mixed, let your dough rest, covered in a wet tea towel.

3. Rest

Resting is a very important step in your bread-making repertoire. This clever idea was discovered by Professor Raymond Clavel of France—he named this process autolysis. Autolysis is the pre-mixing of the flour and water followed by a rest period. Other ingredients are added after this resting period.

Resting allows the flour time to absorb the water fully and allows the gluten to be activated, resulting in a superior dough that is easier to handle (especially the wetter dough which my recipes tend to call for). A resting time of 15-30 minutes is sufficient. A longer time of 25-30 minutes is necessary for wholemeal dough because it takes a longer time for the bran/fibres in the wholemeal flour to absorb water.

Autolysis will allow you to create a dough that has better volume and superior taste by reducing the mixing time, therefore reducing the oxidation of the flours and at the same time saving your arms and shoulders from repetitive strain.

In my own observation, working with sourdough exclusively, it is fine to mix all of the ingredients together: flour, water, starter, salt, prior to the rest/autolyse period. I think this is due to the acidity of sourdough dough.

> **TIPS ADJUST FLOUR OR WATER (IF NECESSARY)**
> If, after the 30-minute rest period your dough still feels wet or too dry, add more water or flour. Add the flour or water by dipping the palm of your hand or fingertips into either the water or flour and then knead it into the dough. Do not add flour or water directly onto the dough because often than not the smallest sprinkling of flour or water is all you need to get the desired consistency.

4. Knead – air knead

Have you ever wondered why we knead the dough for making bread? Kneading transforms the dough from a blob of rough, sticky mass into a smooth, elastic, soft dough. It does this by allowing the gluten to be developed during the process of stretching and folding the dough, a process called 'kneading'. Gluten is the protein storage found in bread-making flour (primarily in wheat and spelt).

Many of the recipes in this book require a wetter dough than you may have experienced. Hence, you may find conventional kneading difficult to do for these wetter doughs. This is where the technique of air kneading is more efficient, where the gluten is developed by literally throwing your dough into the air and then slapping or throwing it onto your work surface. It is best to pick up the dough with your fingertips to avoid the dough sticking to your whole hand. Resist the temptation to add more flour to your dough. After you have kneaded the dough for about 5 minutes, the dough will have become less sticky and will have developed some elasticity.

Once you have adequately kneaded the dough and the dough has passed the windowpane test (see below) successfully, you do not need to repeat the kneading process.

5. Windowpane test

To check whether your dough has had sufficient kneading, you can do a windowpane test by pinching a small amount of dough and then stretching it to create a thin membrane. If your dough can stretch to a thin transparent membrane without tearing, then it is ready. Gather your dough together and try to make a ball.

If not, you need to do more kneading. After 3–5 minutes of kneading, do the windowpane test again, until you have a transparent membrane.

6. Dough retardation

Dough retardation is a process whereby you allow your dough to slow down its rate of fermentation by lowering the temperature when the dough is fermenting. You should do this by placing your dough in the fridge as it will have a constant known low temperature. It is incredibly useful to 'retard' the dough if you are making your dough in warmer temperature (28°C/65°F upwards). It also gives you flexibility, allowing you to rise and bake your bread when you are ready.

The most beneficial effect of dough retardation is the more complex 'sourdough' taste created by lacto-fermentation. At lower temperature, the wild yeast is inhibited from rising the dough too fast, but the lactobacteria flourishes and reproduces faster to give you more organic acids (lactic and acetic acids), creating the pleasant sour taste specific to sourdough.

Dough retardation is not applicable for my gluten-free sourdough recipes or some sourdough recipes. I have clearly indicated in each recipe if dough retardation is useful.

7. Folding or turning the dough

More often than not, the recipe requires you to do a turning/folding process after the first rise or dough retardation. This is a very simple but effective way to 'wake up' the gluten and yeast. It allows the yeast to be invigorated to hold more air and the gluten to re-arrange itself.

You will notice the initial 'soft and slack' dough, after a rise or sleep (dough retardation), will snap out to become 'taut' in a matter of a few turns/folds. Turning/folding is the repeated action of stretching the dough and folding it in half onto itself. After a few turns/folds, the dough will become very taut and tough to stretch/fold. If you force a fold and the dough cracks, it is time to stop folding, as the dough has had enough.

An older bread recipe would ask you to 'punch down or deflate' the dough. We no longer do this movement because it causes the dough to lose all of the air that you have been working in. Turning/folding is most important for wet dough to prevent the dough spreading while it is rising.

8. Divide

Dough needs to be shaped before the final rise. Once shaped, the dough will not spread and will, therefore, have a high volume during the final rise. Shaping your dough is a skill that you will acquire through practice. Dust your bench generously with semolina flour, invert the dough onto the bench and dust the dough with more semolina flour. Divide your dough, if required. Rest the dough for 5–10 minutes so that the gluten can relax.

9. Shape

Shaping your dough requires gentle hands but firm movements—you must not show your hesitation or fear. One thing you need to remember is that your bread will still taste nice even if the shaping is not perfect. You will get better with practice, this is a promise. Do not keep on re-shaping the dough more than a couple of times because you will destroy the integrity of the dough. If you are not sure, bake the dough in a tin, the dough will take the shape of the tin, hiding all the imperfections.

After your dough has rested after the turning, this is the time to shape your dough. It is important to have a light touch when you shape your dough because you do not want to completely rid the loaf of the precious bubbles you have acquired during fermentation.

Here are four basic ways to shape your dough:

1.   SHAPING INTO A ROUND LOAF
   - Flour or oil your bench lightly and gently tip out the dough onto your bench.
   - Cup the piece of dough in both hands
   - Gently rotate the dough while try to tuck in the sides of the dough underneath. This will

become the base of the round loaf.

- As you do this 'rotate and tuck' movement, the dough will become rounder, smoother and tauter.
- Once you have a lovely round shape, turn the dough over and pinch the centre seam tightly
- Place the round loaf centre seam down onto a piece of baking paper.

2.   SHAPING INTO A LONG LOAF

- Flour or oil your bench lightly and gently tip out the dough onto your bench.
- Using the palm of your floured/oiled hands, flatten the dough into an rectangle/elongated oval shape
- Starting from one end of the dough horizontally (the longer side), roll the dough all the way towards the other end. Tuck the overlap underneath and press gently to close the seam.
- Place the long loaf seam side down onto a piece of baking paper.

3.   SHAPING INTO A OVAL LOAF

- Follow instruction for a long loaf, then gently place the palms of your hands on either side of the long loaf.
- Gently roll the loaf backwards and forwards, keeping your hands on the edge of the long loaf.
- Continue this gentle rolling until the ends become tapered.
- Place the loaf seam-side down onto a piece of baking paper.

4.   SHAPING FOR A TINNED LOAF

- For a small tin (10 x 17cm and 10cm deep (4 x 7.5 x 4in)), shape the dough into a round loaf and put it into the tin.
- For a medium tin (10 x 23.5cm and 10cm deep (4 x 9.4 x 4in)), shape the dough into a long loaf and put it into the tin.

NOTE: FOR SHAPING BAGUETTES, SEE RECIPE FOR PARISIAN-STYLE BAGUETTE.

10. Rise

During the life cycle of 'dough to baked bread', the dough needs to rise and double. Most recipes will call for the dough to rise twice, one shorter rise or, alternatively, a slower rise in the fridge (dough retardation) and one longer rise at room temperature. The dough will rise about 25 per cent during the short rise or dough retardation. The long rise is where your dough needs to double, before baking your loaf.

Rising is caused by the wild yeast and lacto bacterial activities. These activities are most

baguettes rising in a tin

prolific when the dough is allowed to rise at a warm room temperature, away from draughts. A rising temperature of 25–28°C (65–83°F) is ideal, but the dough will rise at any temperature above 10°C (25°F), just taking longer time to double. Most importantly, do not use time as your guide because the time for the dough to double will vary, depending on room temperature, humidity, type of flour used and the activity of your starter.

The dough needs to be covered at all times during rising. Cover your rising dough first, with a sheet of baking paper, before you put your wet towel on top of your baking paper.

11. Slashing/scoring the dough

All dough, apart from wet dough such as pizza and ciabatta, requires slashing/scoring. Bread will expand as it bakes, and at some point it will burst and crack. Slashing or scoring your loaf creates a decorative path for the bread to open. Apart from decoration, slashing or scoring is also a useful tool for identifying different types of bread that a baker may produce at one time.

12. Indentation test

To know when your shaped dough has risen enough and ready to bake, you first look to see if the dough has doubled. Once it looks like it has doubled, you do an indentation test. Using the tip of one of your fingers, press your finger gently into the dough. The dough should push back a little but the indentation remains. This means your dough has had sufficient rise and it is now ready for baking. If the indentation disappears, the dough needs more rising time. Do not allow your bread dough to over-rise. Over-rising your bread will cause it to collapse in the oven during baking.

13. Bake

Half an hour before you need to bake your loaves, preheat your oven to the temperature required by the recipe (for most sourdough loaves, this is between 225–235°C (437–455°F)). If you have a granite tile you need to make sure that it is securely placed on top of the lowest rack in your oven before you turn up your oven.

Once your oven is hot and your loaf is ready, place your loaf straight on top of the granite tile, regardless of whether your loaf is free form on baking paper or inside a tin.

You always start by baking the dough on the granite tile, at the bottom of the oven, because dough rises from the bottom. If you need to put in a water bath, always place the water bath on the top rack.

In the first few minutes of baking resist opening your oven as the bread needs the intense heat to create an 'oven spring'. An 'oven spring' is caused by the frantic activity of the yeast—your dough will expand and there will be a huge increase in the size of your loaf.

A pre-heated granite tile really makes a huge difference in creating this 'oven spring', especially when you are baking a wet dough, such as ciabatta. If you cannot find a granite tile, then try to find a couple of fire bricks from your local wood-fired oven manufacturer. A granite tile also improves the heat-retaining quality of an inferior oven.

Usually you need to reduce the oven temperature and move the loaf to a higher rack (middle) to allow the dough to bake further until cooked through. For a heavier loaf, you need to lower the temperature further to allow the inside moisture to be dried away completely without burning the outer crust.

The loaf should be brown/golden brown all over and sound hollow when knocked on the bottom. If you are unsure whether the loaf has cooked through, turn the oven off and let it sit in the oven for a further 5-10 minutes. This will do no harm—instead you will make sure that your crusty crust does not go limp once the bread is out of the oven. Many novice bakers underbake their bread, especially the heavier wholemeal loaf.

It is important to note that heavier, denser dough requires longer baking at a lower temperature (around 180°C/350°F), which will produce a thicker crust. Lighter or wetter dough requires a shorter baking time at a higher temperature (250–275°C/485–527°F) and will have an open crumb and a thin crispy crust. For example, a heavy rye bread will require a long baking time to cook through its interior completely, while ciabatta needs that searing heat to puff and crisp up.

13. Cooling, storing and freezing

Once cooked, take the bread out of the oven (without burning your body parts) and let the bread cool on a wire rack before cutting. Cooling the bread completely, before cutting, is important because the bread continues to cook as it cools down.

Bread should be stored at room temperature, placed inside two paper bags, so the bread can still breathe without going dry too quickly. Bread goes stale and feels dry because the water molecules continue to move from the centre of the loaf (crumb) to the crust. However, reheating by toasting or putting it in the oven for 5 minutes, will reverse the process and redirect the water back to the crumb, making the bread taste fresh again for a short time.

Freezing will keep a loaf of bread fresh for at least a couple of months. You can slice bread prior to putting it into the freezer so that you can just grab a slice or two to toast.

REFRESHING FROZEN SOURDOUGH
To refresh a frozen loaf, take the bread out the freezer until it is completely defrosted, say 4-6 hours; then mist the bread with water all over, bake at 180–200°C (350–400°F) for 10-15 minutes, depending on the size and type of bread you are reheating. A denser loaf will take longer to thaw and crisp up, so use a lower 180°C (350°F) for a dense wholemeal or rye loaf.

OTHER STEPS THAT MAY APPEAR IN SOME RECIPES:

WATER BATHS

A water bath is used when baking crusty loaves such as baguettes or ciabattas. A water bath creates hot steam necessary for this type of bread, where you want to achieve a moist interior with a crusty crust.

To make a water bath, use a shallow baking tray or baking dish. Fill it with boiling water and place it either on the middle or top rack of your oven when baking. A water bath is not necessary for most sourdough loaves in this book—only use one when specified.

Alternatively, you can throw a handful of ice cubes onto the floor of your oven straight after you load your loaves into the hot oven. Ice cubes will sizzle and create hot steam for a few minutes. Misting the loaf prior to baking also helps to create steam.

BASIC SOURDOUGH BREADS

BASIC 'ALMOST' WHITE SOURDOUGH

This is the most basic sourdough loaf, made with white flour, a little rye starter, water and salt. Nothing can be simpler. This is a chewy, complex, satisfying basic loaf for the uninitiated! I have given this loaf a 'sleep' (dough retardation) overnight to give it a longer rise in the warmer months. However, you can let it rise to double straight after kneading and shaping. If you choose to do only one rise, your loaf will be less chewy and less sour, and better for children's sandwiches (this may be a preference for some of you).

INGREDIENTS

ONE LOAF	TWO LOAVES	
100g (3½oz)	200g (7oz)	rye starter culture, ripe and at room temperature
400g (14oz)	800g (1lb 12oz)	organic, unbleached white wheat or spelt flour
240g (8½oz)	480g (17oz)	filtered water, at room temperature
1 ½ teaspoons	3 teaspoons	sea-salt, finely ground

METHOD

MEASURE INGREDIENTS (2–3 MINS): Use, preferably, a digital scale, to weigh all ingredients, including water. Put all ingredients in a non-metallic bowl, starting with water and starter, flour and lastly the salt.

MIX INGREDIENTS (2–3 MINS): Using a spatula or a wooden spoon, stir the ingredients together until they form a cohesive mass.

REST (15–20 MINS)

KNEADING – AIR KNEADING (5 MINS): Using your fingertips, throw your dough into the air and then slap/throw it onto your bench. Repeat this action for about 5 minutes, until the dough has developed some elasticity.

REST (20–30 MINS):As a general rule, 20 minutes rest is sufficient, but, if your dough is still sticky, do a longer rest. This step allows the flour to absorb the water, giving the gluten a chance to realign itself. Your dough should feel soft, elastic and slightly sticky.

DO THE WINDOWPANE TEST: See 'Sourdough Bread Making Step-by-Step'.

FIRST RISE (ABOUT 1 HOUR IN WARM WEATHER AND 2 HOURS IN COLD WEATHER): Leave the dough to rise in a covered container at a comfortable room temperature, around 20–25°C (68–77°F).

DOUGH RETARDATION (OPTIONAL, OVERNIGHT): Cover the dough and leave the dough overnight in the fridge. The next day, take the dough out of the fridge and leave to thaw for about an hour.

PREHEAT YOUR OVEN TO 235°C (455°F)

TURNING/FOLDING: See 'Sourdough Bread Making Step-by-Step'. After turning/folding, let the dough sit for 10–15 minutes to relax the gluten.

DIVIDE AND SHAPE (5 MINS): If you are making two loaves, then weigh and divide the dough into two pieces. Shape the loaves as desired. The single recipe will fit into a small tin or one free form. Double recipe will make two small-tinned loaves or two free-form loaves. Mist the loaves with water and sprinkle with seeds if desired.

SECOND/FINAL RISE (4–6 HOURS AT ROOM TEMPERATURE): Rise the shaped loaves at a comfortable room temperature (around 20–25°C/68–77°F) until almost doubled. Make sure the dough is covered, or mist with water frequently, to prevent drying.

BAKE: Bake for about 10 minutes, then reduce the oven to 215°C (419°F) for a further 25–35 minutes. If you are unsure whether the loaves have cooked through, turn the oven off, and let the loaves sit in the oven for a further 10 minutes.Remove loaves from oven, taking care not to burn yourself!

REST: Let the bread cool before cutting.

SUITABLE FOR FREEZING AND WILL KEEP FOR A COUPLE OF MONTHS FROZEN.

Basic 'Amost' White Sourdough

Basic Wholemeal Sourdough

BASIC WHOLEMEAL SOURDOUGH

If you prefer a more substantial sourdough bread, this wholemeal loaf will give you a very satisfying bread-chewy, nutty and nourishing.
This bread will not rise as much as the basic white bread. The long sourdough fermentation will differentiate this bread from the 'cardboard-like, tasteless' commercial bread and you will be able to taste the wholegrain goodness!

INGREDIENTS

ONE LOAF	TWO LOAVES	
100g (3½oz)	150g (5oz)	rye starter culture, ripe and at room temperature
400g (14oz)	800g (1lb 12oz)	organic wholemeal wheat or spelt flour
260g (9oz)	520g (17½oz)	filtered water, at room temperature
1½ teaspoons	3 teaspoons	sea-salt, finely ground

METHOD

MEASURE INGREDIENTS (2–3 MINS): Use, preferably, a digital scale, to weigh all ingredients, including water. Put all ingredients in a non-metallic bowl, starting with water and starter, flour and lastly the salt.

MIX INGREDIENTS (2–3 MINS): Using a spatula or a wooden spoon, stir the ingredients together until they form a cohesive mass.

REST (15–20 MINS)

KNEADING – AIR KNEADING (5 MINS): Using your fingertips, throw your dough into the air and then slap/throw it onto your bench. Repeat this action for about 5 minutes until the dough has developed some elasticity

REST (20–30 MINS): As a general rule 20 minutes rest is sufficient. However, if your dough is still sticky, do a longer rise—this step allows the flour to absorb the water and gives the gluten a chance to realign itself. Your dough should feel soft, elastic and slightly sticky.

DO THE WINDOWPANE TEST: See 'Sourdough Bread Making Step-by-Step'.

FIRST RISE (ABOUT 1 HOUR IN WARM WEATHER AND 2 HOURS IN COLD WEATHER): Leave the dough to rise in a covered container at a comfortable room temperature, around 20–25°C (68–77°F).

DOUGH RETARDATION (OPTIONAL, OVERNIGHT): Cover the dough and leave the dough overnight in the fridge. The next day, take the dough out of the fridge and leave to come to room temperature for about an hour.

PREHEAT YOUR OVEN TO 235°C (455°F)

TURNING/FOLDING: See 'Sourdough Bread Making Step-by-Step'. After turning/folding, let the dough sit for 10–15 minutes to relax the gluten.

DIVIDE AND SHAPE (5 MINS): If you are using the double recipe, then weigh and divide the dough into two pieces. Shape the loaves as desired. One recipe will fit into a small tin or one free-form loaf. Double recipe will make two small tinned loaves or two free-forms. Mist the loaves with water and sprinkle with seeds, if desired.

SECOND/FINAL RISE (4–6 HOURS AT ROOM TEMPERATURE): Rise the shaped loaves at a comfortable room temperature, around 20–25°C (68–77°F), until almost doubled. Make sure the dough is covered, or mist with water frequently, to prevent drying.

BAKE: Bake for about 10 minutes, then reduce the oven to 215°C (419°F) for a further 25–35 minutes. If you are unsure whether the loaves have cooked through, turn the oven off, and let the loaves sit in the oven for a further 10 minutes. Remove loaves from oven, taking care not to burn yourself!

REST: Let the bread cool before cutting.

SUITABLE FOR FREEZING AND WILL KEEP FOR A COUPLE OF MONTHS FROZEN.

MY EVERYDAY SOURDOUGH

This is my favourite everyday bread-light, but it has the satiating goodness of whole grains. Kamut or coarse semolina flour gives this loaf a beautiful crust.

INGREDIENTS

ONE LOAF	TWO LOAVES	
100g (3½oz)	200g (7oz)	rye or wheat/spelt starter culture, ripe and at room temperature
175g (6oz)	350g (12oz)	organic wholemeal wheat or spelt—preferably stone-ground
175g (6oz)	350g (12oz)	organic white wheat or spelt
50g (1¾oz)	100g (3½oz)	kamut or coarse semolina flour
250g (9oz)	500g (17½oz)	filtered water, at room temperature
1½ teaspoons	3 teaspoons	sea-salt, finely ground
		sesame, poppy or sunflower seeds for sprinkling

METHOD

MEASURE INGREDIENTS (2–3 MINS): Use, preferably, a digital scale, to weigh all ingredients, including water. Put all ingredients in a non-metallic bowl, starting with water and starter, flour and lastly the salt.

MIX INGREDIENTS (2–3 MINS): Using a spatula or a wooden spoon, stir the ingredients together until they form a cohesive mass.

REST (15–20 MINS)

KNEADING – AIR KNEADING (5 MINS): Using your fingertips, throw your dough into the air and then slap/throw it onto your bench. After you have repeated this for about 5 minutes, the dough will have developed some elasticity.

REST (20–30 MINS): As a general rule, 20 minutes rest is sufficient. However, if your dough is still sticky, do a longer rise—this step allows the flour to absorb the water and gives the gluten a chance to realign itself. Your dough should feel soft, elastic and slightly sticky.

DO THE WINDOW PANE TEST: See 'Sourdough Bread Making Step-by-Step'.

FIRST RISE (ABOUT 1 HOUR IN WARM WEATHER AND 2 HOURS IN COLD WEATHER): Leave the dough to rise in a covered container at a comfortable room temperature, around 20–25°C (68–77°F).

DOUGH RETARDATION (OPTIONAL, OVERNIGHT): Cover the dough and leave the dough overnight in the fridge. The next day, take the dough out of the fridge and leave to thaw for about an hour.

PREHEAT YOUR OVEN TO 235°C (455°F)

TURNING/FOLDING: See 'Sourdough Bread Making Step-by-Step'. After turning/folding, let the dough sit for 10–15 minutes to relax the gluten.

DIVIDE AND SHAPE (5 MINS): If you are using the double recipe, then weigh and divide the dough into 2 loaves. Shape the loaves as desired. One recipe will fit into a small tin or will make one free-form. Double recipe will make two small tinned loaves or two free forms. Mist the loaves with water and sprinkle with seeds, if desired.

SECOND/FINAL RISE (4–6 HOURS AT ROOM TEMPERATURE): Rise the shaped loaves at a comfortable room temperature, around 20–25°C(68–77°F), until almost doubled. Make sure the dough is covered, or mist with water frequently, to prevent drying.

BAKE: Bake for about 10 minutes, then reduce the oven to 215°C (419°F) for a further 25–35 minutes. If you are unsure whether the loaves have cooked through, turn the oven off, and let the loaves sit in the oven for a further 10 minutes.Remove loaves from oven, taking care not to burn yourself!

REST: Let the bread cool before cutting.

SUITABLE FOR FREEZING AND WILL KEEP FOR A COUPLE OF MONTHS FROZEN.

My Everyday Sourdough

Parisian-style Baguette

PARISIAN-STYLE BAGUETTE

MAKES 2 BAGUETTES

If you have had the pleasure of walking through the streets of Paris at dawn, you will never forget the aroma of freshly baked bread wafting from every boulangerie. This unique aroma is a side effect of the fava bean flour, an additive that French bakers often put into their flour to both improve its flavour and boost the rising process. In Australia, it is impossible to find fava bean flour, so the alternative is to grind your own. You can substitute with chickpea flour instead or omit the fava bean flour and still have a delicious baguette. I promise you, if you follow this recipe religiously, you will have the elusive French baguette with the incredibly crusty crust and soft interior.

INGREDIENTS

150g (5oz) thin and active white starter culture (1:1 flour to water ratio)
200g (7oz) filtered water, at room temperature
375g (13oz) organic unbleached white wheat

flour (strong gluten flour required)
10g ($^1/_3$oz) fava bean flour or besan flour (chickpea flour) (optional)
1½ teaspoons sea-salt, finely ground

METHOD

MEASURE INGREDIENTS (2–3 MINS): Use, preferably, a digital scale, to weigh all ingredients, including water. Put all ingredients in a non-metallic bowl, starting with water and starter, flour and lastly the salt.

MIX INGREDIENTS (2–3 MINS): Using a spatula or a wooden spoon, stir the ingredients together until they form a cohesive mass.

REST (15–20 MINS): This step allows the flour to absorb the water and activates the gluten.

KNEADING – AIR KNEADING (5–10 MINS): Using your fingertips, throw your dough into the air and then slap/throw it onto your bench. After you have repeated this for about 5 minutes, the dough will be smoother and somewhat less sticky and start to show some elasticity.

REST (20–30 MINS): This dough is not a wet dough—its consistency is slightly stiffer than basic white sourdough. If it is too wet you will not be able to shape it and your baguette will spread as it rises.

KNEAD (5–10 MINS): Knead your dough some more, until your dough is elastic. At this stage, your dough will become difficult to knead. Dough will be smooth.

DO THE WINDOWPANE TEST: See 'Sourdough Bread Making Step-by-Step'.

FIRST RISE (ABOUT 1 HOUR IN WARM WEATHER AND 2 HOURS IN COLD WEATHER): Leave the dough to rise in a covered container, at a comfortable room temperature, around 20-25°C (68-77°F).

DOUGH RETARDATION (2–4 HOURS OR OVERNIGHT): Cover the dough and leave the dough in the fridge. The dough will rise a little in the fridge, about one and a half times its size.

TURNING/FOLDING: After turning/folding, let the dough sit for 10–15 minutes to relax the gluten. See 'Sourdough Bread Making Step-by-Step'.

DIVIDE AND SHAPE: Dust your bench generously with flour then invert the dough onto the bench. Divide the dough into two pieces, round each piece gently with your hand to form tight balls. Rest for about 15 minutes to relax the gluten. Using a rolling pin, roll the ball of dough into an oblong shape of your desired baguette length. Roll the oblong-shaped dough tightly into a baguette shape, place each in a baguette tray. (My baguette tray holds two baguettes.)

FINAL RISE (ABOUT 4 HOURS): Let the baguette rise until double in size.

BAKE: About 30 minutes before the baguette is ready, preheat your oven to 250°C (485°F). Put a large tray on the top rack in the oven. Just before you place the baguette tray in the oven, pour some boiling water on the pre-heated tray or alternatively, throw some ice cubes on the floor of your oven. This will create steam. Score each baguette with a sharp, serrated knife, starting from the tip of the baguette, angle the blade 45 degrees to make three diagonal slashes across the baguette. Place the baguette tray directly on the granite tile at the bottom of a 250°C (485°F) preheated oven for about 7–8 minutes, then reduce to 235°C (455°F) for another 10–12 minutes until golden brown. If you are not sure whether your baguette is cooked or not, leave for another 3–5 minutes—this will do no harm and is better than a baguette with a soggy crust! Remove baguette from oven, taking care not to burn yourself.

CIABATTA PILLOWS

MAKES ABOUT 10 MEDIUM-SIZED CIABATTA PILLOWS

After trying different combinations of flours, I find that this combination of white spelt and white wheat, plus a small amount of kamut or semolina flour, makes simply the best ciabatta. This dough is sticky and I prefer to use my bread maker to knead the dough but you can 'stir' this dough by hand until it comes together and is elastic or you can use your dough mixer. Lucky for us, this wet dough needs no shaping, instead, we will cut this dough into small, rectangular pillows on a bench dusted with lots and lots of flour. Easy peasy!

INGREDIENTS

100g (3½oz) any active starter of your choice, ripe and at room temperature
250g (9oz) organic white wheat
250g (9oz) organic white spelt flour
50g (1¾oz) kamut or coarse semolina flour
360g (12oz) filtered water, at room temperature
2 teaspoons sea-salt, finely ground

METHOD

MEASURE INGREDIENTS (2–3MINS): Use, preferably, a digital scale, to weigh all ingredients, including water. Put all ingredients in a non-metallic bowl, starting with water and starter, flour and lastly the salt.

MIX INGREDIENTS (2–3 MINS): Using a spatula or a wooden spoon, stir the ingredients together until they form a cohesive mass.

REST (20–30 MINS)

STIR (5–10 MINS): Stir this wet dough until it comes together and is almost impossible to stir. This wet dough will eventually become elastic through the stirring. You cannot over-stir this dough by hand. Alternatively use your breadmaker or dough mixer, as per its instruction manual.

FIRST RISE (ABOUT 1 HOUR IN WARM WEATHER AND 2 HOURS IN COLD WEATHER): Leave the dough to rise in a covered container at a comfortable room temperature, around 20–25°C (68–77°F).

DOUGH RETARDATION (OVERNIGHT): Cover the dough and leave the dough overnight in the fridge. The next day, take the dough out of the fridge and leave to thaw for about an hour.

TURNING/FOLDING: See 'Sourdough Bread Making Step-by-Step'. After turning/folding, let the dough sit for 10–15 minutes to relax the gluten.

SECOND/FINAL RISE (4–6 HOURS AT ROOM TEMPERATURE): Rise until almost two and a half times its size, at a comfortable room temperature, around 20–25°C (68–77°F). Make sure the dough is covered, or mist with water to prevent drying. The dough will be full of air bubbles and feel 'squeaky' to your touch.

PREHEAT YOUR OVEN: Place your granite tile on the bottom rack of your oven and proceed to heat your oven to 250–275°C (485–527°F) (fan-forced and bottom heat if possible).

DIVIDE AND SHAPE (5 MINS): Dust your bench generously with flour and load the dough onto the bench. Dust the top of the dough with more flour. Using a dough divider/scraper, divide the dough into 8-10 pieces.

BAKE: Load your 'pillows' onto baking paper first, then transfer them onto the preheated granite tiles to bake for 5 minutes. Move to the middle rack for another for 10 minutes until they are brown and crusty. Spraying with water as you load the 'pillows' will give them a crustier crust.Best eaten warm with loads of butter or dip into your favourite extra virgin olive oil. Enjoy!

SUITABLE FOR FREEZING AND WILL KEEP FOR A COUPLE OF MONTHS FROZEN.

Ciabatta Pillows

Pita Bread

PITA BREAD

MAKES ABOUT 8-10 PITA BREADS

This is the bread for those who love making sandwich wraps or serving with your favourite dip. Pita bread is a flat pocket bread, traditionally cooked on a searing hot, hearth oven. It is a flat round bread, a staple in Lebanon and Egypt. It will puff up like a ball in the hot oven, impressing your children and friends. I find this bread most rewarding~I always surprise my-self with how excited I feel whenever I make it. Pita bread is so more-ish, it is best to make more than you need and freeze some. I also love this bread toasted.

INGREDIENTS

100g (3½oz) white starter culture (made with 1:1 ratio of flour to water)

200g (7oz) atta flour or sifted wholemeal flour

200g (7oz) white flour (wheat or spelt) or you can use all white flour

230–250g (8½oz–9oz) filtered water at room temperature

1 teaspoon fine sea-salt

melted butter or ghee for brushing each pita after it is cooked (optional)

METHOD

MEASURE INGREDIENTS (2–3 MINS): Use, preferably, a digital scale, to weigh all ingredients, including water. Put all ingredients in a non-metallic bowl, starting with water and starter, flour and lastly the salt.

MIX INGREDIENTS (2–3 MINS): Using a spatula or a wooden spoon, stir the ingredients together until they form a cohesive mass.

REST (15–20 MINS)

KNEADING – AIR KNEADING (5 MINS): Using your fingertips, throw your dough into the air and then slap/throw it onto your bench. After you have repeated this for about 5 minutes, the dough will have developed some elasticity.

REST (20–30 MINS): Your dough should feel soft, elastic and not sticky at all. Let it rest in a covered, non-metallic container or a bowl covered with a wet tea towel or cling wrap.

DO THE WINDOWPANE TEST: See 'Sourdough Bread Making Step-by-Step'.

FIRST RISE (ABOUT 3–4 HOURS): Let your dough rise until one and a half times its original size (the time taken will vary).

TURNING/FOLDING: See 'Sourdough Bread Making Step-by-Step'. After turning/folding, let the dough sit for 10–15 minutes to relax the gluten.

PREHEAT YOUR OVEN: Place your granite tile on the bottom rack of your oven and proceed to heat your oven to 250–275°C (485–527°F) (fan-forced and bottom heat if possible).

DIVIDE AND SHAPE (5 MINS): Divide the dough with a dough scraper into 8–10 portions (75–80g/2 ½oz). Roll each piece into a ball. Using a small rolling pin, roll each piece into a round disk of 10–12cm (4–6ins) and dust with more flour on both sides. Then roll again until it is thin and about 15cm (6ins) in diameter. Slap your pita between your palms to remove excess flour.

BAKE: Put pita bread directly onto your granite stone or the bottom of your preheated oven. In a few minutes, the dough will puff up, magically separating into two layers. Immediately take out of the oven and keep wrapped in tea towels (to keep the pita bread soft). Best eaten warm (you can also toast it to warm it up). Alternatively, you can move the cooked pita onto the higher rack and let the pita dry out—this crunchy pita is great for serving with dips.

SUITABLE FOR FREEZING AND WILL KEEP FOR A COUPLE OF MONTHS FROZEN.

100 % Rye Loaf

ANCIENT WHOLE GRAINS:

RYE, BARLEY, SPELT AND KAMUT

HEAVY RYE SPELT SANDWICH LOAF

MAKES 2 SMALL-TINNED LOAVES

Almost all commercial rye bread is made with less than 10 per cent rye flour (the rest is wheat), even though it may look very dark. The dark colour is achieved by using a colouring agent, such as roasted malt, roasted barley, coffee or, if you are unlucky, artificial caramel. This recipe is created for those of you who love the dark earthy taste of rye but prefer the lighter texture of a soft sandwich loaf. But don't be fooled, this rye sourdough bread has about 35 per cent rye flour. The small amount of vegetable oil will make the dough easier to handle and will give the loaf a softer crumb.

RECIPE NOT SUITABLE FOR DOUGH RETARDATION METHOD

INGREDIENTS

500g (17½ oz) white spelt starter culture, ripe and at room temperature

350g (12oz) filtered water at room temperature

300g (10½oz) organic wholemeal rye

350g (12oz) organic unbleached white spelt (high-gluten content preferable)

2 tablespoons extra virgin olive oil or any vegetable oil of your choice

3 teaspoons sea-salt, finely ground

METHOD

MEASURE INGREDIENTS (2–3 MINS): Use, preferably, a digital scale, to weigh all ingredients including water. Put all ingredients in a non-metallic bowl, starting with water and starter, flour and lastly the salt.

MIX INGREDIENTS (2–3 MINS): Using a spatula or a wooden spoon, stir the ingredients together until they form a cohesive mass. Make sure the dough is well mixed, with no bits of dry flour. This dough is wet and sticky, somewhat pasty.

REST (15–20 MINS): This step is most important for this dough, allowing a greater absorption of water.

KNEADING – AIR KNEADING (5–10MINS): Using your fingertips, throw your dough into the air and then slap/throw it onto your bench. After you have done this for about 5–10 minutes, your dough should feel soft and somewhat 'elastic'. It does not have the elasticity of wheat or spelt dough, but the dough should not be lifeless and pasty. It must a have a little bounciness.Do not over-knead as your dough will be even stickier.

REST (20–30 MINS)

DIVIDE AND SHAPE (5 MINS): Oil your bench and hands. Divide the dough into two equal pieces (about 750g/24oz). Shape each dough piece into a round shape, the best way you can and place each ball of dough into the small bread tin. This dough is difficult to shape as it is sticky and has little elasticity. Do not worry too much, it will take the shape of the tin as it rises. Spray the top of the loaf with water and sprinkle with some rye flour or poppy seeds. As the dough rises and bakes in the oven, it will crack and form beautiful patterns with the flour or seed topping.

FIRST AND FINAL RISE (4–6 HOURS): Let your dough rise until it reaches almost the top of the tin and the surface of the loaf has started to crack. Do not over-rise, as your loaf will collapse in the oven. It is best to err on the under-risen side if you are not sure. Make sure you are watching this dough as it can rise very quickly towards the end of its rising time.

PREHEAT YOUR OVEN TO 235°C (455°F)

BAKE: Bake for about 10 minutes, then reduce the oven to 185°C (365°F) for a further 45–55 minutes until cooked through. Turn the oven off and leave the two loaves for an extra 10–15 minutes. Remove from oven, taking care not to burn yourself!

REST: Let the bread cool before cutting.

SUITABLE FOR FREEZING AND WILL KEEP FOR A COUPLE OF MONTHS FROZEN.

Heavy Rye Spelt Sandwich Loaf

My Pumpernickle

MY PUMPERNICKLE

MAKES 1 SMALL-TINNED LOAF (HIGH RISE) OR
1 MEDIUM-TINNED LOAF (WILL RISE TO ABOUT THE TOP OF THE TIN)

I love the flavour of authentic pumpernickel bread. This loaf has all of the complex flavour of pumpernickel without the heaviness of real pumpernickel bread. It is still a dense heavy rye loaf containing about 45 per cent rye wholemeal flour. This bread is fragrant with ground caraway and fennel seed, and dark in colour with a mysterious complex flavour due to the addition of chocolate, coffee, prune and molasses. No one will ever guess what's in this bread!

RECIPE NOT SUITABLE FOR DOUGH RETARDATION METHOD

INGREDIENTS

200g (7oz) rye starter culture, ripe and at room temperature

250g (9½oz) filtered water, at room temperature

50g (1 ¾oz) freshly brewed espresso coffee, cooled

30g (1oz) dark molasses

5 teaspoons butter, melted or softened or oil

5 pitted prunes, finely chopped

20g ($^2/_3$oz) cocoa powder

200g (7oz) organic wholemeal rye

280–300g (10–10½oz) organic unbleached white spelt (high-gluten content preferable)

1 teaspoon finely ground caraway seed

½ teaspoon finely ground fennel seed

2 teaspoons sea-salt, finely ground

METHOD

MEASURE INGREDIENTS (2–3 MINS): Use, preferably, a digital scale, to weigh all ingredients including water. Put all ingredients in a non-metallic bowl, starting with the liquids followed by pitted prunes, flours and spices and lastly the salt.

MIX INGREDIENTS (2–3 MINS): Using a spatula or a wooden spoon, stir the ingredients together until they form a cohesive mass and all ingredients are evenly distributed. Make sure the dough is well mixed, with no bits of dry flour. This dough is wet and sticky, somewhat pasty.

REST (15–20 MINS): This step is most important for this dough, allowing a greater absorption of water

KNEADING – AIR KNEADING (5–10 MINS): Using your fingertips, throw your dough into the air and then slap/throw it onto your bench. After you have done this for about 5-10 minutes, your dough should feel soft and somewhat 'elastic'. It does not have the elasticity of wheat or spelt dough, but the dough should not be lifeless and pasty. It must a have a little bounciness. Do not over-knead as your dough will be even stickier.

REST (20-30 MINS)

SHAPE (5 MINS): Oil your bench and hands. Shape dough into a log shape, the best way you can. Place shaped dough into the small/medium bread tin. This dough is difficult to shape as it is sticky and has little elasticity. Do not worry too much, it will take the shape of the tin as it rises. Spray the top of the loaf with water and sprinkle with some rye flour or caraway seeds.

FIRST AND FINAL RISE (4–6 HOURS): Let your dough rises until it reaches almost the top of the tin. Do not over-rise, as your loaf will collapse in the oven. It is best to err on the under-risen side if you are not sure. Make sure you are watching this dough as it can rise very quickly towards the end of its rise.

PREHEAT YOUR OVEN TO 235°C (455°F)

BAKE: Bake for about 10 minutes, then reduce the oven to 185°C (365°F) for a further 1 hour to 1 hour 15 minutes, until cooked through. Turn the oven off and leave the loaf for an extra 10-15 minutes. Remove loaf from oven, taking care not to burn yourself! This pumpernickel loaf has a very dark brown colour, which can mislead you into thinking this loaf is overcooked/burnt, when it is not. It is best to slightly over-cook than under-cook this dense bread.

REST: Let the bread cool before cutting.

SUITABLE FOR FREEZING AND WILL KEEP FOR A COUPLE OF MONTHS FROZEN.

100% RYE OR RYE & OAT WHOLEGRAIN SOURDOUGH

MAKES 1 MEDIUM LOAF (WILL NOT FILL TIN COMPLETELY) OR 1 FREE-FORM LOAF

This grainy, chewy, tangy, earthy bread is made entirely from rye—both rye flour and cracked rye grain are used. For those readers who have asked me for 100 per cent rye sourdough, this recipe is for you! You need to soak the rye grain a day or two before. If you can not find cracked rye, you can replace cracked rye with steel cut oats for a delicious variation.

My favourite way to eat this bread is with paté and gherkins, however a thick slather of goat cheese, topped with Seville orange marmalade works equally well.

RECIPE NOT SUITABLE FOR DOUGH RETARDATION METHOD

INGREDIENTS

SOAK
170g (6oz) cracked rye or steel cut oats
250g (9oz) boiling hot water, cooled to about 50°C (122°F)

Place cracked rye in a bowl and pour the hot water over it. Mix well and let soak for 12–24 hours.

DOUGH
All of the soaked rye
250g (9oz) rye starter culture, ripe and at room temperature
400g (14oz) filtered water, at room temperature
255g (9oz) organic wholemeal rye

1 teaspoon finely ground caraway seed (optional)
2 teaspoons sea-salt, finely ground
60g (2oz) egg white (optional, but it adds body to this loaf)

METHOD

MEASURE INGREDIENTS (2–3 MINS): Use, preferably, a digital scale, to weigh all ingredients including water. Put all ingredients in a non-metallic bowl, starting with liquids: water and starter, egg white (if using), followed by flour, ground caraway seed, all of the soaker and lastly the salt.

MIX INGREDIENTS (2–3 MINS): Using a spatula or a dough scraper, mix the ingredients together until they form a cohesive mass. Make sure this sticky dough is well mixed, with no bits of dry flour. This dough is wet and sticky, somewhat pasty.

REST (15–20 MINS): This step is most important for this dough, allowing a greater absorption of water.

SHAPE (5 MINS): Oil your bench and hands. Using a dough scraper, shape dough into a log shape, the best way you can. This dough is difficult to shape as it is sticky and has no elasticity. Do not worry too much, it will take the shape of the tin as it rises. If you like, you can roll this log in a mixture of two-thirds crushed rye grain and one-third rye flour. Place shaped dough into the medium bread tin.

FIRST AND FINAL RISE (4–6 HOURS): Let your dough rise until it is over one and a half its original size and the surface of the loaf has started to crack. Do not wait until this dough doubles as it will collapse before your eyes. Like all heavy rye loaves, do not over-rise, as your loaf will collapse in the oven. It is best to err on the under-risen side if you are not sure. Make sure you are watching this dough as it can rise very quickly towards the end of its rise.

PREHEAT YOUR OVEN TO 215°C (419°F)

BAKE: Bake for about 15 minutes, then reduce the oven to 170°C (338°F) for a further 1 hour 15 minutes to 1 hour 30 minutes until cooked through. Turn the oven off and leave the loaf for an extra 10-15 minutes. Remove loaves from oven, taking care not to burn yourself!

REST: Let the bread cool before cutting.

SUITABLE FOR FREEZING AND WILL KEEP FOR A COUPLE OF MONTHS FROZEN.

Rye & Oat Wholegrain Sourdough

Rye & Buckwheat Loaf

RYE & BUCKWHEAT OR RYE & BARLEY LOAF

MAKES 1 MEDIUM-TINNED LOAF (IT WILL RISE TO ALMOST THE TOP OF THE TIN)
(WHEAT AND SPELT FREE)

This is a delicious wholemeal loaf–its flavour somewhat sweet and earthy. This recipe was created for one of my students, who can eat only rye, barley or oats. Many people find the lighter texture of this wholemeal loaf surprising. Barley gives the loaf a lighter colour and flavour than the buckwheat rye loaf, and a slight sweetness. Barley also does not have the bitterness that buckwheat has. If you would like a 100 per cent barley bread, you can replace the rye starter with a barley starter. In Perth, I can get barley kernels or barley flour grown biodynamically from the ancient stock. It is different to modern barley as the wheat threshes its husk when it matures. The benefit of this is that you can have milled flour the whole kernel, without it being processed by 'pearling'. You can slice this bread thinly for sandwiches.

RECIPE NOT SUITABLE FOR DOUGH RETARDATION METHOD

INGREDIENTS

275g (9½oz) rye starter culture, ripe and at
    room temperature
200g (7oz) filtered water at room temperature
200g (7oz) organic wholemeal rye flour
200g (7oz) organic buckwheat or barley flour
100g (3½oz) potato flour
1 teaspoon finely ground caraway seed

1 teaspoon finely ground fennel seeds
2 teaspoons sea-salt, finely ground

OPTIONAL:
30g (1oz) rice malt or barley, for extra
    sweetness
20g (²/₃oz) vegetable oil, for softness

METHOD

MEASURE INGREDIENTS (2–3 MINS): Use, preferably, a digital scale, to weigh all ingredients including water. Put all ingredients in a non-metallic bowl, starting with the water and starter, rice malt (if using) then the rest of the ingredients and lastly the salt.

MIX INGREDIENTS (2–3 MINS): Using a spatula or a wooden spoon, stir the ingredients together until they form a cohesive mass. Make sure the dough is well mixed, with no bits of dry flour. This dough is wet and sticky, somewhat pasty.

REST (15–20 MINS): This step is most important for this dough, allowing a greater absorption of water.

KNEADING – AIR KNEADING (5–10 MINS): Using your dough scraper, throw your dough into the air and then slap/throw it onto your bench. Do this 'kneading' for about 5–10 minutes. Your dough is sticky and somewhere between a thick batter and a very wet dough. Do not over-knead as your dough will be even stickier.

REST (20–30 MINUTES)

SHAPE (5 MINS): Oil your bench and hands. Shape dough into a round shape, the best way you can. Place shaped dough into the medium bread tin. This dough is difficult to shape as it is sticky and has no elasticity. Do not worry, it will take the shape of the tin as it rises. Spray the top of the loaf with water and sprinkle with some rye flour or seeds. As the dough rises and bakes in the oven, it will crack and form beautiful patterns with the flour or seeds topping.

FIRST AND FINAL RISE (4–6 HOURS): Let your dough rise until it reaches almost the top of the tin (one and a half times its original size) and the surface of the loaf has started to crack. Do not over-rise, as your loaf will collapse in the oven. It is best to err on the under-risen side if you are not sure. Make sure you are watching this dough as it can rise very quickly towards the end of its rise.

PREHEAT YOUR OVEN TO 235°C (455°F)

BAKE: Bake for about 10 minutes, then reduce the oven to 185°C (365°F) for a further 1 hour to 1 hour 15 minutes until cooked through. Turn the oven off and leave the loaf for an extra 10–15 minutes. Remove loaf from oven, taking care not to burn yourself!

REST: Let the bread cool before cutting.

SUITABLE FOR FREEZING AND WILL KEEP FOR A COUPLE OF MONTHS FROZEN.

RYE SPELT APPLE LOAF WITH FENNEL SEEDS

MAKES 1 MEDIUM-TINNED LOAF

This is a really gorgeous rye fruit loaf. It is a heavy, moist and earthy loaf. You can substitute ground fennel with ground cardamon for a different aroma. If you like a sweeter or more fruity loaf, you can add 100-150g (3 ½oz-5oz) of sultanas, chopped apricots or figs, or a mixture of these.

RECIPE NOT SUITABLE FOR DOUGH RETARDATION METHOD

INGREDIENTS

200g (7oz) rye starter culture, ripe and at room temperature
200g (7oz) apple juice
20g (²/₃oz) apple juice concentrate
135g (4½oz) organic wholemeal rye
200g (7oz) organic unbleached white spelt

(high-gluten content preferable)
75–100g (2½–3½oz) dried apple rings or apricots, chopped
1 teaspoon finely ground fennel seed or ground cardamon
2 teaspoons sea-salt, finely ground

METHOD

MEASURE INGREDIENTS (2–3 MINS): Use, preferably, a digital scale, to weigh all ingredients including water. Put all ingredients in a non-metallic bowl, except chopped apple rings, starting with apple juice and starter, apple juice concentrate, flour, ground fennel seed and lastly the salt.

MIX INGREDIENTS (2–3 MINS): Using a spatula or a wooden spoon, stir the ingredients together until they form a cohesive mass. Make sure the dough is well mixed, with no bits of dry flour. This dough is wet and sticky, somewhat pasty.

REST (15–20 MINS): This step is most important for this dough, allowing a greater absorption of water.

KNEADING – AIR KNEADING (5–10 MINS): Using your fingertips, throw your dough into the air and then slap/throw it onto your bench. After you have done this for about 5–10 minutes, your dough should feel soft and somewhat 'elastic'. It does not have the elasticity of wheat or spelt dough, but the dough should not be lifeless and pasty. It must a have a little bounciness. Do not over-knead as your dough will be even stickier.

REST (20–30 MINS)

ADD: Add chopped apple rings and knead into the dough, making sure they are distributed well.

SHAPE (5 MINS): Oil your bench and hands. Shape dough into a log shape, the best way you can. Place shaped dough into the medium bread tin. This dough is difficult to shape as it is sticky and has little elasticity. Do not worry too much, it will take the shape of the tin as it rises.

FIRST AND FINAL RISE (4–6 HOURS): Let your dough rise until it reaches almost the top of the tin. Do not over-rise, as your loaf will collapse in the oven. It is best to err on the under-risen side if you are not sure. Make sure you are watching this dough as it can rise very quickly towards the end of its rise.

PREHEAT YOUR OVEN TO 225°C (437°F)

BAKE: Bake for about 10 minutes, then reduce the oven to 185°C (365°F) for a further 1 hour to 1 hour 15 minutes until cooked through. Turn the oven off and leave the loaf for an extra 10–15 minutes. Remove loaf from oven, taking care not to burn yourself!

REST: Let the bread cool before cutting.

SUITABLE FOR FREEZING AND WILL KEEP FOR A COUPLE OF MONTHS FROZEN.

Rye Spelt Apple Loaf with Fennel Seeds

Kamut & Spelt Sandwich Loaf

KAMUT & SPELT SANDWICH LOAF

MAKES 1 MEDIUM-TINNED LOAF

This golden sandwich loaf is delicious and has a beautiful crust. I love Kamut for its nutty taste and it adds crustiness to any bread. Kamut is one of the ancient wheat grains and, according to plant geneticists, its DNA does not contain the gene that causes allergic reactions to coeliacs. You need to start 6-12 hours before to make the Kamut sourdough starter.
NOTE: This recipe has white spelt containing gluten.

RECIPE NOT SUITABLE FOR DOUGH RETARDATION METHOD

INGREDIENTS

300g (10½oz) active kamut starter culture (made with a tablespoon of active rye starter, 150g (5oz) kamut flour and 150g (5oz) water)

280g (10oz) filtered water, at room temperature

200g (7oz) organic kamut flour (replace with fine semolina if kamut is unavailable)

300g (7oz) organic unbleached white spelt (high gluten content preferable)

2 teaspoons sea-salt, finely ground

METHOD

MEASURE INGREDIENTS (2–3 MINS): Use, preferably, a digital scale, to weigh all ingredients including water. Put all ingredients in a non-metallic bowl, starting with water and starter, flours and lastly the salt.

MIX INGREDIENTS (2–3 MINS): Using a spatula or a wooden spoon, stir the ingredients together until they form a cohesive mass. Make sure the dough is well mixed, with no bits of dry flour.

REST (15–20 MINS): This step is most important for this dough, allowing a greater absorption of water

KNEADING – AIR KNEADING (5–10 MINS): Using your fingertips, throw your dough into the air and then slap/throw it onto your bench. After you have done this for about 5–10 minutes. You may find it easier to oil your bench and your hands. Your dough should feel soft and slightly sticky. This is an elastic dough.

REST (20–30 MINS): As a general rule, 20 minutes rest is sufficient. However, if your dough is still sticky, do a longer rise—this step relaxes the gluten and gives the gluten strands a chance to re-align.

SHAPE (5 MINS): Sprinkle some kamut flour onto your bench. Shape dough into a log shape. Place shaped dough into the medium bread tin. Spray the top of the loaf with water and sprinkle with some kamut flour.

FIRST AND FINAL RISE (3-5 HOURS): Let your dough rise until it reaches almost the top of the tin and the surface of the loaf starts to crack. Make sure you are watching this dough as it can rise very quickly towards the end of its rise.

PREHEAT YOUR OVEN TO 235°C (455°F)

BAKE: Bake for about 10 minutes, then reduce the oven to 200°C (365°F) for a further 35–45 minutes until cooked through. Remove loaf from oven, taking care not to burn yourself!

REST: Let the bread cool before cutting.

SUITABLE FOR FREEZING AND WILL KEEP FOR A COUPLE OF MONTHS FROZEN.

CRUSTY KAMUT LOAF

MAKES 1 MEDIUM FREE-FORM LOAF

Kneading this loaf will give you great pleasure as this golden dough is soft and elastic. Once baked, this dough will reward you with a golden crusty loaf, reminding you of an Italian crusty semolina loaf. You need to start 6-12 hours before to make the kamut sourdough starter. For variations, before shaping add some fresh corn kernels and cheddar cheese. This is the perfect bread to eat with any soups, especially a delicious corn chowder!

RECIPE NOT SUITABLE FOR DOUGH RETARDATION METHOD

INGREDIENTS

500g (17½oz) active kamut starter culture (made with a tablespoon of active rye starter, 250g (9oz) kamut flour and 250g (9oz) water)

300g (10½oz) organic unbleached white spelt flour (high gluten, if possible)
2 teaspoons sea-salt, finely ground

METHOD

MEASURE INGREDIENTS (2–3 MINS): Use, preferably, a digital scale, to weigh kamut starter and flour. Put kamut starter, flour and salt in a non-metallic bowl.

MIX INGREDIENTS (2-3 MINS): Using a spatula or a wooden spoon, stir the ingredients together until they form a cohesive mass. Make sure the dough is well mixed, with no bits of dry flour.

REST (15–20 MINS): This step is most important for this dough, allowing a greater absorption of water.

KNEADING – AIR KNEADING (5–10 MINS): Using your fingertips, throw your dough into the air and then slap/throw it onto your bench. After you have done this for about 5–10 minutes, your dough should feel soft, elastic and not sticky.

SHAPE (5 MINS): Sprinkle some kamut flour on your bench. Shape dough into a round or a log. Place shaped dough onto baking paper. Spray the top of the loaf with water and pack some kamut flour on top of the loaf.

FIRST AND FINAL RISE (3–5 HOURS): Let your dough rise until it doubles. The surface of the loaf will start to crack. Make sure you are watching this dough as it can rise very quickly towards the end.

PREHEAT YOUR OVEN TO 235°C (455°F)

BAKE: Bake for about 10 minutes, then reduce the oven to 200°C (400°F) for a further 25–35 minutes until cooked through. Remove loaf from oven, taking care not to burn yourself!

REST: Let the bread cool before cutting.

SUITABLE FOR FREEZING AND WILL KEEP FOR A COUPLE OF MONTHS FROZEN.

Crusty Kamut Loaf

Golden Linseed & Kamut Loaf

GOLDEN LINSEED & KAMUT LOAF

MAKES 1 MEDIUM-TINNED LOAF

Golden linseed and the golden coloured kamut marry well together, creating a crusty loaf with a delicious nuttiness. This is one of my favourite sourdoughs. You need to start 6-12 hours before, to make the kamut sourdough starter.

RECIPE NOT SUITABLE FOR DOUGH RETARDATION METHOD

INGREDIENTS

500g (17½oz) kamut starter culture, ripe
   and at room temperature (made with a
   tablespoon of active rye starter, 250g (9oz)
   kamut flour and 250g (9oz) water)
300g (10½oz) organic unbleached white spelt

flour (high gluten, if possible)
50g (1¾oz) golden linseed meal (ground
   golden linseeds)
2 teaspoons sea-salt, finely ground

METHOD

MEASURE INGREDIENTS (2–3 MINS): Use, preferably, a digital scale, to weigh both kamut starter, flour and linseed meal. Put kamut starter, flour and salt in a non-metallic bowl.

MIX INGREDIENTS (2–3 MINS): Using a spatula or a wooden spoon, stir the ingredients together until they form a cohesive mass. Make sure the dough is well mixed, with no bits of dry flour.

REST (15–20 MINS): This step is most important for this dough, allowing a greater absorption of water.

KNEADING – AIR KNEADING (5–10 MINS): Using your fingertips, throw your dough into the air and then slap/throw it onto your bench. After you have done this for about 5–10 minutes, your dough should feel soft, elastic and not sticky. Add linseed meal and knead in well to distribute.

SHAPE (5 MINS): Sprinkle some kamut flour onto your bench. Shape dough into a round or a log. Place shaped dough onto baking paper. Spray the top of the loaf with water and sprinkle with some linseed meal.

FIRST AND FINAL RISE (3–5 HOURS): Let your dough rise until it doubles. The surface of the loaf will start to crack. Make sure you are watching this dough as it can rise very quickly towards the end of its rise.

PREHEAT YOUR OVEN TO 235°C (455°F)

BAKE: Bake for about 10 minutes, then reduce the oven to 200°C (400°F) for a further 25–35 minutes until cooked through. Remove loaf from oven, taking care not to burn yourself!

REST: Let the bread cool before cutting.

SUITABLE FOR FREEZING AND WILL KEEP FOR A COUPLE OF MONTHS FROZEN.

My Everyday Sandwich Loaf

GLUTEN-FREE
SOURDOUGH

BROWN RICE BREAD

MAKES 1 SMALL-TINNED LOAF (GLUTEN FREE)

This is the simplest gluten-free loaf, you can even omit the ground linseed in the starter if it does not agree with you. It was my first success with gluten-free sourdough, using a brown rice starter. The loaf will rise and crack, almost like a normal loaf. It has a beautiful moist crumb, somewhere between a loaf and a cake and cuts and keeps well. It is better to freeze the loaf in slices, then you can toast it straight away without having to thaw it out. I prefer this bread toasted. This loaf has a high protein content, due to the high quantity of egg whites used, lowering the GI index and keeping you full for longer.

INGREDIENTS

750g (24oz) active brown rice/linseed starter
125g (4oz) egg white (about 3-4 eggs)
85g (3oz) brown rice flour

100g (3½oz) potato flour
1 teaspoon sea-salt
2 teaspoons raw sugar (optional)

METHOD

MEASURE INGREDIENTS (2–3 MINS): Use, preferably, a digital scale, to weigh all ingredients. Put all ingredients in a non-metallic bowl, starting with all the liquid (e.g. starter, egg white, water if using) then the rest of the ingredients and lastly, salt and sugar.

BEAT/WHISK INGREDIENTS (2–3 MINS): Using an electric whisk or a hand beater, whisk the ingredients together until mixed well and fluffy, about 2–3 minutes.

REST (30 MINS): After 30 minutes, if the batter has become too thick, adjust its consistency by adding water by the tablespoon. The texture should be like a sponge cake or thick pancake batter.

POUR YOUR BATTER INTO TIN (3–5 MINS): Line the tin with non-stick paper or oil it if you are not using a non-stick tin. Whisk the batter again for a couple of seconds, then pour into the small tin. Spray top surface with water. Sprinkle with seeds, if you wish. Cover with a plastic lid or an upside-down container.

FIRST AND FINAL RISE (3–4 HOURS OR CAN BE LONGER DEPENDING ON AMBIENT TEMPERATURE): Let your dough rise to just over one and a half times its size—the time taken will vary. Do not over-rise—if the batter is over-risen, it will deflate as you move the tin into the oven.

PREHEAT YOUR OVEN TO 200°C (400°F)

BAKE: Bake for about 10 minutes, then reduce the oven to 180°C (350°F) for a further 1 hour and 15 minutes until browned and cooked. Test with a wooden skewer, if you wish. If you are unsure whether the loaf has cooked through, turn the oven off, and let the loaves sit in the oven for a further 20–30 minutes. This will do no harm, as all gluten-free loaves have a moist crumb. Remove loaves from oven, taking care not to burn yourself!

REST: Let the bread cool completely before cutting. All gluten-free bread is best cut with a sharp un-serrated, thin-bladed knife (I use my very sharp and thin-bladed Chinese cleaver!).

SUITABLE FOR FREEZING AND WILL KEEP FOR A COUPLE OF MONTHS FROZEN.

Brown Rice Bread

Buckwheat Linseed Bread with Caraway Seed

BUCKWHEAT LINSEED BREAD WITH CARAWAY SEED

MAKES 1 SMALL-TINNED LOAF (GLUTEN FREE)

This loaf is my triumph! It was worth all of the loaves I had to throw out and many frustrating days of failures. This gluten-free bread is the closest to a 'fluffy, light' commercial yeasted bread (nothing short of a miracle). And yet, it is made with nutrient-dense wholegrain buckwheat flour, ground linseed and a small amount of potato flour to lighten the texture. Ground caraway seed gives this loaf an aromatic (like caraway rye bread) fragrance, somewhat camouflaging the strong buckwheat smell most people find unpleasant.

INGREDIENTS

450g (15½ oz) active buckwheat starter
60g (2oz) egg white
100g (3½ oz) potato flour
3 tablespoons golden linseed, ground

1 teaspoon sea salt
2 teaspoons raw sugar (optional)
1 teaspoon caraway seed powder

METHOD

MEASURE INGREDIENTS (2-3 MINS): Use, preferably, a digital scale, to weigh all ingredients. Then put all ingredients in a non-metallic bowl, starting with all the liquid (e.g. starter, egg white) then the rest of the ingredients and lastly, the salt and sugar.

BEAT/WHISK INGREDIENTS (2-3 MINS): Using an electric whisk or a hand beater, whisk the ingredients together until they are mixed well and fluffy, about 2-3 minutes.

REST (30 MINS): After 30 minutes, if the batter has become too thick, adjust its consistency by adding water by the tablespoon. The texture should be like a sponge cake or thick pancake batter.

POUR YOUR BATTER INTO TIN (3-5 MINS): Line the tin with non-stick paper or oil it if you are not using a non-stick tin. Whisk the batter again for a couple of seconds, then pour into the small tin (10 x 17cm (4 x 7.5in) and 10cm (4in) high). Spray top surface with water. Sprinkle with seeds, if you like. Cover with a plastic lid or an upside-down container.

FIRST AND FINAL RISE (3-4 HOURS OR CAN BE LONGER DEPENDING ON AMBIENT TEMPERATURE): Let your dough rise to just over one and a half times its size—the time taken will vary. Do not over-rise—if the batter is over-risen, it will deflate as you move the tin into the oven.

PREHEAT YOUR OVEN TO 200°C (400°F)

BAKE: Bake for about 10 minutes, then reduce the oven to 180°C (350°C) for a further 1 hour and 15 minutes until browned and cooked. Test with a wooden skewer, if you wish. If you are unsure whether the loaf has cooked through, turn the oven off, and let it sit in the oven for a further 20-30 minutes. This will do no harm, as all gluten-free loaves have a moist crumb. Remove loaf from oven, taking care not to burn yourself!

REST: Let the bread cool completely before cutting. Best cut with a sharp un-serrated thin bladed knife (I use my very sharp and thin-bladed Chinese cleaver!).

SUITABLE FOR FREEZING AND WILL KEEP FOR A COUPLE OF MONTHS FROZEN.

MULTIGRAIN GLUTEN-FREE BREAD

MAKES 1 SMALL TINNED LOAF (VEGAN, EGG FREE)

This loaf is my second triumph. It has more body than the Buckwheat Linseed Bread-it cuts well and in my opinion, it is the best gluten-free bread for making sandwiches. This loaf is suitable for vegans, as it contains no eggs.

INGREDIENTS

350g (12oz) buckwheat/sorghum starter
90g (3½oz) quinoa flour
90g (3½oz) potato flour

1 teaspoon sea-salt
2 teaspoons raw sugar (optional)

METHOD

MEASURE INGREDIENTS(2–3 MINS): Use, preferably, a digital scale, to weigh all ingredients. Put all ingredients in a non-metallic bowl, starting with all the liquid (e.g. starter) then the rest of the ingredients and lastly, salt and sugar.

BEAT/WHISK INGREDIENTS (2–3 MINS): Using an electric or hand whisk or beater, whisk the ingredients together until well-mixed and fluffy.

REST (30 MINS): After 30 minutes, if the batter has become too thick, adjust its consistency by adding water by the tablespoon. The texture should be like a sponge cake or thick pancake batter.

POUR YOUR BATTER INTO TIN (3–5 MINS):
Line the tin with non-stick paper or oil it if you are not using a non-stick tin. Whisk the batter again for a couple of seconds, then pour into a small tin. Spray top surface with water. Sprinkle with seeds, if you like. Cover with a plastic lid or an upside-down container.

FIRST AND FINAL RISE (3–4 HOURS OR CAN BE LONGER DEPENDING ON AMBIENT TEMPERATURE): Let your dough rise to just over one and a half times its size—the time taken will vary. Do not over-rise—if the batter is over-risen, it will deflate as you move the tin into the oven.

PREHEAT YOUR OVEN TO 200°C (400°F)

BAKE: Bake for about 10 minutes, then reduce the oven to 180°C (350°F) for a further 1 hour and 15 minutes until browned and cooked. Test with a wooden skewer, if you wish. If you are unsure whether the loaf has cooked through, turn the oven off, and let it sit in the oven for a further 20–30 minutes. This will do no harm, as all gluten-free loaves have a moist crumb. Remove loaf from oven, taking care not to burn yourself!

REST: Let the bread cool completely before cutting. All gluten-free bread is best cut with a sharp un-serrated thin-bladed knife (I use my very sharp and thin bladed Chinese cleaver!).

SUITABLE FOR FREEZING AND WILL KEEP FOR A COUPLE OF MONTHS FROZEN.

Multigrain Gluten-free Bread

Buckwheat Sorghum Bread

BUCKWHEAT SORGHUM BREAD

MAKES 1 SMALL-TINNED LOAF (GLUTEN FREE)

This is one of the simplest gluten-free loaves. I was asked by one of my students, who suffers allergies to quinoa and linseed, as well as being coeliac, to create a loaf without any of those ingredients. This loaf is nowhere near as light as the Multigrain or Buckwheat Linseed with ground caraway seed, but it has a moist cakey crumb. However, it cuts well and tastes nice. For me, this loaf tastes best when it is toasted.

INGREDIENTS

500g (17½oz) active buckwheat/sorghum
   starter
200g (7oz) potato flour

60g (2oz) egg white (from about 2 eggs)
1 teaspoon sea-salt
2 teaspoons raw sugar

METHOD

MEASURE INGREDIENTS (2–3 MINS): Use, preferably, a digital scale, to weigh all ingredients. Then put all ingredients in a non-metallic bowl, starting with all the liquid (e.g. starter, egg white) then the rest of the ingredients and lastly, the salt and sugar.

BEAT/WHISK INGREDIENTS (2–3 MINS): Using an electric or hand whisk or beater, whisk the ingredients together until they are well mixed and fluffy.

REST (30 MINS): After 30 minutes, if the batter has become too thick, adjust the water by adding water by the tablespoon. The texture should be like a sponge cake or thick pancake batter (thick but pourable).

POUR YOUR BATTER INTO TIN (3–5 MINS): Line the tin with non-stick paper or oil it if you are not using a non-stick tin. Whisk the batter again for a couple of seconds and then pour into a small tin. Spray top surface with water. Sprinkle with seeds, if you like. Cover with a plastic lid or an upside-down container.

FIRST AND FINAL RISE (3–4 HOURS OR CAN BE LONGER DEPENDING ON AMBIENT TEMPERATURE): Let your dough rise to just over one and a half times its size—the time taken will vary. Do not over-rise—if the batter is over-risen, it will deflate as you move the tin into the oven.

PREHEAT YOUR OVEN TO 200°C (400°F)

BAKE: Bake for about 10 minutes, then reduce the oven to 180°C (350°F) for a further 1 hour and 15 minutes until browned and cooked. Test with a wooden skewer, if you wish. If you are unsure whether the loaf has cooked through, turn the oven off, and let it sit in the oven for a further 20–30 minutes. This will do no harm, as all gluten-free loaves have a moist crumb. Remove loaf from oven, taking care not to burn yourself!

REST: Let the bread cool completely before cutting. Best cut with a sharp un-serrated thin-bladed knife (I use my very sharp and thin-bladed Chinese cleaver!).

SUITABLE FOR FREEZING AND WILL KEEP FOR A COUPLE OF MONTHS FROZEN.

BROWN RICE SORGHUM BREAD

MAKES 1 SMALL-TINNED LOAF (GLUTEN FREE)

This loaf is buckwheat-free for those who do not like buckwheat. It makes a great sandwich loaf as it cuts nicely. I like its simplicity and mild taste. Egg whites give this loaf a high protein content and its bread-like crumb. The loaf is not as light as the buckwheat-based gluten-free loaves.

INGREDIENTS

500g (17½oz) brown rice/linseed starter
120g (4oz) potato flour
100g (3½oz) sorghum flour

90g (3oz) egg white (from about 3 eggs)
1 teaspoon sea-salt
2 teaspoons raw sugar (optional)

METHOD

MEASURE INGREDIENTS (2–3 MINS): Use, preferably, a digital scale, to weigh all ingredients. Put all ingredients in a non-metallic bowl, starting with all the liquid (e.g. starter, egg white) then the rest of the ingredients and lastly, salt and sugar.

BEAT/WHISK INGREDIENTS (2–3 MINS):
Using an electric or hand whisk or beater, whisk the ingredients together until they are well mixed and fluffy.

REST (30 MINS):
After 30 minutes, if the batter has become too thick, adjust the water by adding it by the tablespoon. The texture should be like a sponge cake or thick pancake batter (thick but pourable).

POUR YOUR BATTER INTO TIN (3–5 MINS): Line the tin with non-stick paper or oil it if you are not using a non-stick tin. Whisk the batter again for a couple of seconds and then pour into a small tin. Spray top surface with water. Sprinkle with seeds, if you like. Cover with a plastic lid or an upside-down container.

FIRST AND FINAL RISE (3–4 HOURS OR CAN BE LONGER DEPENDING ON AMBIENT TEMPERATURE): Let your dough rise to just over one and a half times its size—the time taken will vary. Do not over-rise—if the batter is over-risen, it will deflate as you move the tin into the oven.

PREHEAT YOUR OVEN TO 200°C (400°F)

BAKE: Bake for about 10 minutes, then reduce the oven to 180°C (350°F) for a further 1 hour and 15 minutes until browned and cooked. Test with a wooden skewer, if you wish. If you are unsure whether the loaves have cooked through, turn the oven off, and let the loaves sit in the oven for a further 20–30 minutes. This will do no harm, as all gluten-free loaves have a moist crumb. Remove loaves from oven, taking care not to burn yourself!

REST: Let the bread cool completely before cutting. All gluten-free bread is best cut with a sharp un-serrated thin-bladed knife (I use my very sharp and thin-bladed Chinese cleaver!).

SUITABLE FOR FREEZING AND WILL KEEP FOR A COUPLE OF MONTHS FROZEN.

Brown Rice Sorghum Bread

My Everyday Sandwich Loaf

MY EVERYDAY SANDWICH LOAF

MAKES 1 SMALL-TINNED LOAF (GLUTEN FREE)

This is my favourite gluten-free loaf. It rises well and produces a lovely, fluffy, light bread that cuts well and tastes nice. It is very special to me because unlike all the commercial gluten-free bread I have tasted, this loaf is not heavy, crumbly or cakey and its crumb is the closest to normal (gluten) bread. I am very pleased to give you an easy recipe that is nourishing for your health, as it is made with whole grains. My pleasure will be complete if you enjoy and make this beautiful loaf over and over again.

INGREDIENTS

400g (14oz) active buckwheat sorghum starter
60g (2oz) egg white
100g (3½oz) potato flour
100g (3½oz) quinoa flour

1 teaspoon sea-salt
2 teaspoons raw sugar (optional)
1 teaspoon caraway or fennel seed powder (optional)

METHOD

MEASURE INGREDIENTS (2–3 MINS):
Use, preferably a digital scale, to weigh all ingredients. Put all ingredients in a non-metallic bowl, starting with all the liquid (e.g. starter, egg white, water if using) then the rest of the ingredients and lastly, salt and sugar.

BEAT/WHISK INGREDIENTS (2–3 MINS): Using an electric or hand whisk or beater, whisk the ingredients together until well mixed and fluffy.

REST (30 MINS): After 30 minutes, if the batter becomes too thick, adjust the water by adding it by the tablespoon. The texture should be like a sponge cake or thick pancake batter.

POUR YOUR BATTER INTO TIN (3–5 MINS): Line the tin with non-stick paper or oil it if you are not using a non-stick tin. Whisk the batter again for a couple of seconds and then pour into a small tin. Spray top surface with water. Sprinkle with seeds, if you like. Cover with an upside-down plastic lid or container.

FIRST AND FINAL RISE (3–4 HOURS OR CAN BE LONGER DEPENDING ON AMBIENT TEMPERATURE): Let your dough rises to just over one and a half times its size—the time taken will vary. Do not over-rise—if the batter is over-risen, it will deflate as you move the tin into the oven.

PREHEAT YOUR OVEN TO 200°C (400°F)

BAKE: Bake for about 10 minutes, then reduce the oven to 180°C (350°F) for a further 1 hour and 15 minutes until browned and cooked. Test with a wooden skewer, if you wish. If you are unsure whether the loaf has cooked through, turn the oven off, and let it sit in the oven for a further 20–30 minutes. This will do no harm, as all gluten-free loaves have a moist crumb. Remove loaf from oven, taking care not to burn yourself!

REST: Let the bread cool completely before cutting. All gluten-free bread is best cut with a sharp un-serrated thin-bladed knife (I use my very sharp and thin-bladed Chinese cleaver!).

SUITABLE FOR FREEZING AND WILL KEEP FOR A COUPLE OF MONTHS FROZEN.

Coconut Gluten-free Waffles

COCONUT GLUTEN-FREE WAFFLES

ONE RECIPE MAKES 4-6 WAFFLES (DAIRY FREE)

This recipe is created for those of you who love coconut! It is simply the most amazing coconut sourdough waffle: light, crisp and very coconutty. It is really beautiful served with banana, a drizzle of palm sugar syrup and a scoop or two of coconut or vanilla bean ice-cream. The good news is that it is dairy-free and gluten-free. Also, it is so good for you because it uses nourishing whole brown rice flour, not highly processed starch. My wonderful tester, Tania (who is not a coeliac), was very impressed by how light these waffles were, with almost no difference in texture to wheat waffles. Well worth the effort to make a few batches at a time, as they can be frozen and reheated in a toaster or a hot oven. Make sure you oil your waffle maker well so your waffles don't stick.

INGREDIENTS

STEP 1: START 6-12 HOURS PRIOR TO MAKING THE WAFFLE BATTER
25g (¾oz) brown rice starter

200g (7oz) brown rice flour

200g (7oz) coconut milk

Mix well and leave, covered, in a warm place. This starter mixture should have a consistency of a very thick double cream. It is ready when the starter mixture has risen and is mousse-like, about 12 hours. The surface does not look bubbly but if you use a spatula to pry the thick liquid underneath, you will see a mousse-like mixture.

STEP 2: MAKING THE WAFFLE BATTER
300g (10½oz) active brown rice starter from step 1, there will be some left over

70g (about 2 large eggs) egg white

½ teaspoon sea-salt

1 teaspoon raw organic sugar (optional)

½ teaspoon bicarbonate soda

additional coconut milk or mineral water if mixture is too thick

MEASURE INGREDIENTS (2–3 MINS): Use, preferably, a digital scale, to weigh all ingredients. Put all ingredients in a non-metallic bowl, starting with eggs, starter then the rest of the ingredients and lastly, salt.

MIX INGREDIENTS (3 MINS): Using a hand/electric whisk, whisk all ingredients together for 3 minutes until well mixed. The mixture will look like bubbly single cream.

COOK THE WAFFLES: Heat up a cast-iron waffle iron. Make sure you butter or oil your pan generously to prevent sticking, just before you add the batter. If using an electric waffle maker, follow the manufacturer's instructions. Wait till the waffle iron is hot but not smoky. Spray waffle iron with olive oil or butter spray, which will stop the waffle from sticking. Pour the waffle batter to about half of the height of the waffle iron. Reduce heat to half. Do not over-fill as the batter will over-flow and make a very sticky mess to clean. Let cook for about 3–5 minutes, until cooked and golden brown. After a couple of waffles, you will work out how much batter to use and how long to cook the waffle. Repeat the process until all the batter is used. Eat immediately while they are still warm.

BUCKWHEAT CRÊPES

RECIPE MAKES 10 CRÊPES (EGG FREE)

Buckwheat makes the laciest and fluffiest crêpes, which will please anyone, even children and non-coeliacs. Use water if you want to have a 'crunchier' crêpe. Milk will give a tender crumb.

INGREDIENTS

STEP 1: START 6-12 HOURS PRIOR TO MAKING THE BATTER

25g (¾oz) buckwheat starter (or any other gluten-free starter you have)

200g (7oz) buckwheat flour
200g (7oz) milk (or water)

Mix well, and leave covered in a warm place. This starter mixture should have a consistency of a thick pancake batter. It is ready when the starter mixture is mousse-like or bubbly.

STEP 2: MAKING THE CRÊPE BATTER

400g (14oz) active starter from step 1
1 teaspoon salt
200g (7oz) milk (or water)

2 teaspoons raw organic sugar (optional)
add extra water/milk if mixture is too thick

METHOD

MEASURE INGREDIENTS (2–3 MINS): Use, preferably, a digital scale, to weigh all ingredients. Put all ingredients in a non-metallic bowl.

MIX INGREDIENTS (3 MINS): Using a hand/electric whisk, whisk all ingredients together for 3 minutes until well mixed. The mixture should be the consistency of a thin single cream, if not, whisk in more milk.

COOK THE CRÊPES: Heat up a crêpe pan or a shallow sauté pan if you do not have a crêpe pan. Heat up 1-2 teaspoons of melted butter until very hot. Pour 2-3 tablespoons of batter into the crêpe pan, turn and rotate the pan so the batter covers the whole surface of the pan. Cook until the crêpe is browned, about 2-3 minutes. Toss the crêpe or turn with a flat silicon or wooden spatula and brown the other side (about 1 minute). Transfer to a plate and keep warm. Repeat the process until all batter is used. Eat immediately while still warm.

Buckwheat Crêpes

Buckwheat Blinis

BUCKWHEAT BLINIS

RECIPE MAKES APPROXIMATELY 25 BLINIS (EGG FREE)

These lovely soft blinis are great with sour cream and caviar (or whatever you prefer).

INGREDIENTS

STEP 1: 6-12 HOURS PRIOR TO MAKING THE BLINI BATTER

25g (¾oz) buckwheat starter

200g (7oz) milk (or water)

200g (7oz) buckwheat flour

Mix well, and leave covered in a warm place. This starter mixture should have a consistency of a thick pancake batter. It is ready when the starter mixture is bubbly or mousse-like.

STEP 2: MAKING THE BLINI BATTER

400g (14oz) active starter from step 1

2 teaspoons raw organic sugar (optional)

1 teaspoon sea-salt

½ teaspoon bicarbonate soda

125g (4oz) milk (or water)

additional milk or mineral water if too thick

METHOD

MEASURE INGREDIENTS (2–3 MINS): Use, preferably, a digital scale, to weigh all ingredients. Put all ingredients in a non-metallic bowl.

MIX INGREDIENTS (3 MINS): Using a hand/electric whisk, whisk all ingredients together for three minutes until well mixed. The mixture should be the consistency of thick pancake batter, if not, whisk in more milk or water.

COOK THE CREPES: Heat up a crepe pan or a shallow sauté pan. Heat up 1–2 teaspoons of melted butter until very hot. Pour 1–1 1/2 tablespoons of blini batter on the hot pan. This will spread slightly into a small round blob. Adjust the amount of mixture if you want a slightly larger blini. Continue to add several blobs of mixture until pan is full, but not overcrowded. Cook until the blinis in the pan are browned, about 2–3 minutes. Turn the blinis with a flat silicon or wooden spatula and brown the other side (about 1 minute). Transfer to a plate and keep warm. Repeat the process until all batter is used. Eat immediately while they are stillwarm or can be cooled to enjoy with savoury toppings.

BUCKWHEAT OR BROWN RICE GLUTEN-FREE CRUMPETS

MAKES 8 10CM-ROUND CRUMPETS (EGG FREE, DAIRY FREE, VEGAN)

This gluten-free crumpet is simply awesome—it rises well and the buckwheat version's pliable crumb makes it perfect to hold fillings for sandwiches or burgers. You can sprinkle these crumpets with some sesame seeds to imitate burger buns. It is soft and fluffy and also child friendly! A brown rice crumpet's texture is a little crumbly and doesn't hold a filling very well. NOTE: See chapter on Equipment for information and a picture of a suitable crumpet ring.

INGREDIENTS

STEP 1: 6-12 HOURS PRIOR TO MAKING THE CRUMPET BATTER

50g (1¾oz) active gluten-free starter of your choice (buckwheat or brown rice/linseed)

300g (10½oz) gluten-free flour or your choice (buckwheat or brown rice)

500–550g (17½–19oz) filtered water (lukewarm water if the weather is cold)

Mix well and leave covered in a warm place. This starter mixture should have a consistency of a thick pancake batter. It is ready when the starter mixture is bubbly. If the mixture is too thick then stir in a small amount of additional water to attain the correct consistency.

STEP 2: MAKING THE CRUMPET BATTER

600g (21oz) active starter from step 1

1 teaspoon salt

2 teaspoons raw organic sugar (optional)

1 teaspoon bicarbonate soda

50g (1¾oz) melted butter for cooking the crumpets

additional milk or mineral water if mixture is too thick

METHOD

MIX INGREDIENTS (2–3 MINS): Using a hand/electric whisk, briefly whisk all ingredients together. The mixture will be frothy and will look like pourable cream.

COOK THE CRUMPETS: Heat up a cast-iron griddle or sauté pan. If using a normal cast-iron pan, make sure you butter or oil your pan generously to prevent sticking just before you add the batter to the pan. I find that if I butter the pan whilst it is heating up the butter tends to burn. Prepare each crumpet ring by smearing its side generously with butter/oil. Place the crumpet rings on the pan. Wait till the pan and the rings are hot but not smoky, about 10 minutes. Pour the crumpet batter to about two-thirds of the height of the ring. Reduce the heat to medium–low. Let cook for about 8–10 minutes, during which time small bubbles will appear all over the surface of the crumpet. The crumpet is ready to be flipped when the top surface of the crumpet looks translucent or cooked, leaving a 1–2 cm (½–¾in) area of raw batter in the middle of the crumpet. The side will shrink a little and pull away from the ring. Remove ring from each crumpet. Once flipped, cook the crumpet for a further 2–3 minutes until golden on the surface. Traditionally crumpet is eaten toasted to give it extra crunchiness.

SUITABLE FOR FREEZING AND WILL KEEP FOR A COUPLE OF MONTHS FROZEN.

Buckwheat Crumpet

Brown Rice Crumpet

Sourdough Coconut Kaffir Lime Cake

SOURDOUGH COCONUT KAFFIR LIME CAKE

MAKES 2 SQUARE CAKES OF 15 X 15CM (6IN) AND ABOUT 6-7CM (2 ½-2¾INS) HIGH

I owe my mum for this recipe and for showing me seven times how to make this cake! When I first made it, it tasted beautiful but it didn't have the texture that it should have. We finally figured out that to get the right texture we needed to use fresh, boiled coconut milk. All tinned or tetra packed liquid coconut milk or coconut cream, organic and non-organic, has been processed or thickened with an emulsifier and will not curdle or separate into a top layer of oily coconut cream and a bottom layer of coconut milk, which you need for this recipe to work. However, even when it takes the texture of a pudding, the taste and aroma of this cake is heavenly. NOTE: You will need white sand for this recipe, available from your local hardware store.

INGREDIENTS

STEP 1: START 12 HOURS PRIOR TO MAKING THE CAKE BATTER

50g (1¾oz) active brown rice starter
300g (10½oz) organic brown rice flour

400ml (13½fl oz) coconut milk (canned variety is fine)

Mix well and leave covered in a warm place. This starter mixture should have the consistency of a very thick double cream. It is ready when the starter mixture has risen and become mousse-like, about 12 hours. The surface does not look bubbly but if you use a spatula to pry the thick liquid out from underneath, you will see a mousse-like mixture.

STEP 2: MAKING THE CAKE BATTER

150g (5oz) bubbly active starter, from step 1 (there will be some left over)
125g (4oz) egg yolks, about 6-7 large eggs
250g (9oz) raw caster sugar
3-5 kaffir lime leaves (optional, can be substituted with 1 teaspoon of vanilla bean

paste)
500ml (17fl oz) cooked and curdled, oily coconut milk *see comment above
250g (9oz) tapioca flour
1 teaspoon (salt)

METHOD

MEASURE INGREDIENTS (2-3 MINS): Use, preferably, a digital scale, to weigh all ingredients separately. Ground raw caster sugar with kaffir lime until it becomes icing sugar.

MIX INGREDIENTS (3 MINS): Using a hand/electric whisk, whisk all raw sugar/kaffir lime mixture with the egg yolk and salt for three minutes until it is thick and white. The mixture will look like thick cream. In alternating small quantities, add in the oily, cooked coconut milk and tapioca flour. Lastly, pour in the brown rice starter and mix well so there are no lumps.

FIRST AND FINAL RISE UNTIL DOUBLED (ABOUT 2–5 HOURS): Rise the cake batter, covered, at a comfortable room temperature around 20–25°C (68–77°F), making sure the batter is well covered. The batter will rise a little and become frothy.

COOK THE CAKE: Pour some clean white sand into the bottom of a deep roasting cast-iron pan. The sand needs to be measured and levelled to about 2cm (1in) deep. Heat up the sand on the stove top, on medium heat for at least 15–20 minutes before baking. Whisk the batter again, then pour the cake batter to about half of the height of the square tin. Do not over-fill as the batter will over-flow and make a very difficult sticky mess to clean. Let the cake cook for about 20–25 minutes, you will see bubbles appearing on two-thirds of the surface of the cake. In the meantime, preheat your oven to 180°C (350°F). Take the cake off the heat and put it into the oven to finish the cooking process. Use a bamboo skewer to test if the cake is cooked in the middle (the bamboo skewer should come out clean). This will take about 15 minutes.

COOK THE CAKE: Let the cake cool for 10–15 minutes in the tin. Take the cake out of the tin and let it cool completely before cutting.

sand under the baking tin.

BUCKWHEAT BEETROOT CHOCOLATE CAKE

MAKES 1 SQUARE CAKE MEASURING 15 X 15CM (6INS)
AND ABOUT 5-6CM (2-2½INS)

Chocolate goes really well with buckwheat. Somehow, each flavour enhances the other. I have added a small amount of grated apple or beetroot to add moisture and texture to the cake. Do not stress, the cake will only rise about one and a quarter times but it will spring up more in the oven. This is a deliciously dense and intense chocolate brownie. You would not guess it is gluten-free and is made of wholegrain buckwheat! See 'European' doughnut recipe for the ganache.

INGREDIENTS

200g (7oz) active buckwheat starter
115g (4oz) sorghum flour
115g (4oz) potato flour
50g (1¾oz) best quality cocoa powder
200g (7oz) organic raw caster sugar
1 teaspoon vanilla extract

75g (1¾oz) beetroot (or apple, if you prefer), finely grated
75g (2½oz) melted butter
3 large organic eggs
1 teaspoon sea-salt, finely ground

METHOD

MEASURE INGREDIENTS (2–3 MINS): Prepare the tin by buttering and lining the bottom and sides of the cake tin with non-stick baking paper. Preheat the oven to 180°C (350°F). Measure ingredients and keep aside. In a non-metallic bowl, sift and mix the flours and cocoa together. Add the cooled melted butter and starter.

MIX INGREDIENTS: In a separate bowl, cream the eggs, sugar and salt until fluffy. Add the flour and cocoa mixture into the egg sugar mixture, vanilla extract and grated beetroot/apple. Whisk ingredients well until they are thoroughly combined, about three minutes. Let the batter sit for about 20 minutes. Whisk again for a couple of minutes.

FIRST AND FINAL RISE: Pour the cake batter into the lined tin and cover the surface with a wet tea towel or cling wrap. Let the cake rise until it has risen about one and a quarter times larger than its original size. This will take a while and the time taken will vary. (In my cool kitchen, about 20–23°C (70–80°F), it took, on average, 4–6 hours for my cake to rise.) An increase in volume will occur during baking, so do not worry if you can't see if the cake has risen or not.

PREHEAT YOUR OVEN TO 180°C (350°F)

COOK THE CAKE: Bake for about 20 minutes then reduce heat to 165°C (329°F) and bake for an extra 45–60 minutes and test with a skewer at about 45–50 minutes. If the skewer comes out clean, then it is cooked. If not, put it back in the oven.

COOK THE CAKE: Let the cake cool for 5–10 minutes in the tin. Take the cake out of the tin and let it cool completely before cutting. Glaze with chocolate ganache or icing, if desired. Best served warm.

Buckwheat Beetroot Chocolate Cake

HIGH PROTEIN
HIGH FIBRE
LOW GI
SOURDOUGH
BREADS

LUPIN & SUNFLOWER SEED LOAF

MAKES 2 LOAVES (MY PREFERENCE) OR 1 MEDIUM-TINNED LOAF

Sweet lupin flour is a practically pure protein and high fibre gluten-free flour. Australian sweet lupin (*Lupinus angustifolius*) differs from the European lupin, which contains a high percentage of poisonous alkaloids. Sweet lupin, however, still contains small amounts of the toxic alkaloids and anti-nutrients (protease inhibitor). Long sourdough fermentation or sprouting is vital to make lupin more digestible for our bodies. Using sweet lupin in long and slow fermented sourdough bread will further reduce the GI index. Sweet lupin has a slight 'beany' and bitter taste that can be unpleasant to some people. Toasted sweet lupin flour smells delicious and is easy to do you can toast the flour lightly on a shallow pan with constant stirring to prevent burning.

INGREDIENTS

150g (5oz) white or wholemeal spelt culture, ripe and at room temperature

450–475g (15½–16oz) filtered water, at room temperature

125g (4oz) sweet lupin flour (chickpea/besan flour if sweet lupin can't be found)

475g (16oz) organic unbleached white spelt flour

2 teaspoons sea-salt, finely ground

SUNFLOWER SEEDS MIXTURE

1 cup sunflower seeds

3 teaspoons tamari (gluten free) or naturally fermented soya sauce

METHOD

MAKE THE SUNFLOWER SEEDS MIXTURE: Mix the sunflower seeds with the tamari/soy sauce in a bowl, then spread them on an oven tray and toast for 15–20 minutes at 175ºC (350ºF) until they are crispy. You need to toss the seeds around to make sure they toast evenly. Cool the seed mixture completely before grinding half of the seeds into flour in your food processor.

MEASURE INGREDIENTS (2–3 MINS): Use, preferably, a digital scale, to weigh all ingredients including water. Put all ingredients in a non-metallic bowl, starting with water and starter, flours, including the sunflower seed flour, and lastly the salt.

MIX INGREDIENTS (2–3 MINS): Using a spatula or a wooden spoon, stir the ingredients together until they form a cohesive mass.

REST (30 MINS): This longer resting time is necessary for the water-hungry lupin flour.

KNEADING – AIR KNEADING (5 MINS): Using your fingertips, throw your dough into the air and then slap/throw it onto your bench. After you have done this for about 5 minutes, the dough will have developed some elasticity. If your dough feels dry and hard, add some water by misting all around the dough, and let it absorb the water for 10–15 minutes before re-kneading to incorporate the water.

REST (20–30 MINS): Your dough should feel soft and elastic, not hard and dry.

DO THE WINDOWPANE TEST: See 'Sourdough Bread Making Step-by-Step'.

FIRST RISE (ABOUT 1 HOUR IN WARM WEATHER AND 2 HOURS IN COLD WEATHER): Leave the dough to rise in a covered container, for about 1–2 hours, at a comfortable room temperature, around 20–25°C(68–77°F).

TURNING/FOLDING: See 'Sourdough Bread Making Step-by-Step'. After turning/folding, let the dough sit for 10–15 minutes to relax the gluten.

ADD: Add in the sunflower seed mixture and knead lightly to distribute the seeds evenly.

DIVIDE AND SHAPE (5 MINS): You can either make one medium-sized loaf or two small ones. Divide and shape the loaves as desired. Mist the loaf/loaves with water and sprinkle with extra seeds if desired.

SECOND/FINAL RISE (4–6 HOURS AT ROOM TEMPERATURE): Rise the shaped loaf/loaves until almost doubled, at a comfortable room temperature, around 20–25°C (68–77°F). Make sure the dough is covered, or mist with water frequently, to prevent drying.

PREHEAT YOUR OVEN TO 225°C (437°F)

BAKE: Bake for about 10 minutes, then reduce the oven to 205°C (400°F) for a further 25–35 minutes until cooked, depending on the size of your loaf/loaves. If you are unsure whether the loaves have cooked through, turn the oven off, and let the loaves sit in the oven for a further 10 minutes. Remove loaves from oven, taking care not to burn yourself!

REST: Let the bread cool before cutting.

SUITABLE FOR FREEZING AND WILL KEEP FOR A COUPLE OF MONTHS FROZEN.

Lupin & Sunflower Seed Loaf

Lupin Pita Bread

LUPIN PITA BREAD

This lupin pita bread has an incredibly delicious aroma of caramel. As I have explained in the Sourdough Pita Bread recipe, making this bread is extremely rewarding especially if you are in the centre of a crowd of children and adults. Everyone's eyes will light up when the flat dough magically puffs up in the oven. It is not worth making a small (half recipe) batch because you will be making quite a bit of a mess on your kitchen bench. Most people will be very happy to help you roll out the dough, especially curious children (and nice adults).

INGREDIENTS

150g (5oz) white or wholemeal spelt starter culture, ripe and at room temperature
400–425g (15½–16oz) filtered water, at room temperature
125g (4oz) sweet lupin flour (or chickpea/besan flour if sweet lupin can't be found)

475g (16oz) organic unbleached white spelt or high gluten (11–12 per cent) white premium bakers flour
2 teaspoons sea-salt, finely ground
Melted butter or ghee for brushing after each pita is cooked (optional)

METHOD

MEASURE INGREDIENTS (2–3 MINS): Use, preferably, a digital scale, to weigh all ingredients, including water. Put all ingredients in a non-metallic bowl, starting with water and starter, flour and lastly the salt.

MIX INGREDIENTS (2–3MINS): Using a spatula or a wooden spoon, stir the ingredients together until they form a cohesive mass.

REST (15–20 MINS)

KNEADING – AIR KNEADING (5 MINS): Using your fingertips, throw your dough into the air and then slap/throw it onto your bench. After you have done this for about 5 minutes, the dough will have developed some elasticity.

REST (20–30 MINS): As a general rule, 20 minutes rest is sufficient. Your dough should feel soft, elastic and not sticky at all. Gather your dough together and try to make a ball, let it rest in a non-metallic container or a bowl, covered with a wet tea towel or cling wrap.

FIRST RISE (ABOUT 3–4 HOURS): Let your dough rises until one and a half times its original size—the time taken will vary.

TURNING/FOLDING: See 'Sourdough Bread Making Step-by-Step'. After turning/folding, let the dough sit for 10–15 minutes to relax the gluten.

DIVIDE AND SHAPE (5 MINS): Divide the dough with a dough scraper into 14–15 portions (75–80g/2 ½oz). Roll each piece into a ball. Using a small rolling pin, roll each ball into a round disk of 10–12cm (4–5ins) and dust with more flour on both sides. Then roll again until it is thin and about 15cm (6ins) in diameter. Slap your pita between your palms to remove excess flour.

PREHEAT YOUR OVEN: Place your granite tile on the bottom rack of your oven and preheat your oven to 250–275°C (485–527°F), fan-forced and bottom heat if possible.

BAKE : Once oven is hot, put pita bread directly on your granite stone or the bottom of your oven. In a few minutes, the dough will puff up, magically separating into two layers. Immediately take out of the oven and keep wrapped in tea towels (to keep the pita bread soft). Best eaten warm (you can also toast it to warm it up).Alternatively, you can move the cooked pita onto the higher rack and let the pita dry out—this crunchy pita is great for serving with dips.

SUITABLE FOR FREEZING AND WILL KEEP FOR A COUPLE OF MONTHS FROZEN.

SOURDOUGH CRUSTY CHESTNUT KAMUT LOAF

MAKES 2 SMALL LOAVES

Chestnut adds a sweet taste and aroma to this basic spelt sourdough bread. Apart from its delicious taste, chestnut adds protein, fibres, vitamin B and folate. Italians use chestnut flour extensively in their cakes and desserts (monte bianco). Freeze-dried chestnut flour, if you can find it, is a better-quality flour since it retains its nutritional contents. Kamut or semolina flour gives this loaf a crusty crust, like the Italian semolina breads. The crumb of this loaf is dark, dense and satisfyingly chewy.

INGREDIENTS

150g (5oz) white or wholemeal spelt starter culture, ripe and at room temperature
280-300g (10-10½oz) filtered water, at room temperature
100g (3½oz) chestnut flour

100g (3½oz) kamut flour or semolina flour
300g (10½oz) organic unbleached white spelt or high gluten (11–12 per cent) white premium bakers flour
1 teaspoon sea-salt, finely ground

METHOD

MEASURE INGREDIENTS (2–3 MINS): Use, preferably, a digital scale, to weigh all ingredients, including water. Put all ingredients in a non-metallic bowl, starting with water and starter, flour and lastly the salt.

MIX INGREDIENTS (2–3 MINS): Using a spatula or a wooden spoon, stir the ingredients together until they form a cohesive mass.

REST (15–20 MINS)

KNEADING (10–15 MINS): This non-sticky dough can be kneaded normally using the heel of your hand. Using the heel of your hand fold the dough onto itself, then do a quarter turn. Repeat the action of folding and turning until the dough becomes smooth and elastic. After you have done this for about 10–15 minutes, the dough will have developed some elasticity and be smooth.

REST (20–30 MINS): This dough needs this 20–30 minute rest to allow the chestnut and kamut flour to absorb the water.

FIRST RISE (ABOUT 1 HOUR IN WARM WEATHER AND 2 HOURS IN COLD WEATHER): Leave the dough to rise in a covered container, at a comfortable room temperature, around 20–25°C (68–77°F).

TURNING/FOLDING: See 'Sourdough Bread Making Step-by-Step'. After turning/folding, let the dough sit for 10–15 minutes to relax the gluten.

DIVIDE AND SHAPE (5 MINS): Divide the dough into two and shape the loaves as desired. Mist the loaves with water. Pack some spelt flour on top of the loaves. The dough will crack as it rises and bakes, and this flour will create decorative cracks on top of the dough.

SECOND/FINAL(RISE 4-6 HOURS AT ROOM TEMPERATURE): Rise the shaped loaves until almost doubled at a comfortable room temperature, around 20-25°C (68-77°F). Make sure the dough is covered, or mist frequently with water, to prevent drying.

PREHEAT YOUR OVEN TO 225°C (437°F)

BAKE: Bake for about 10 minutes, then reduce the oven to 205°C (400°F) for a further 20–25 minutes. If you are unsure whether the loaves have cooked through, turn the oven off, and let the loaves sit in the oven for a further 10 minutes. Remove loaves from oven, taking care not to burn yourself!

REST: Let the bread cool before cutting.

SUITABLE FOR FREEZING AND WILL KEEP FOR A COUPLE OF MONTHS FROZEN.

Sourdough Crusty Chestnut Kamut Loaf

Quinoa Spelt Sourdough Loaf

QUINOA SPELT SOURDOUGH LOAF

MAKES 2 SMALL LOAVES

Quinoa is a gluten-free flour that has the added benefit of having a very high protein content. Quinoa also adds a lot of sponginess to the dough, a rarity for a gluten-free flour, and a nutty taste to the bread. Black or red quinoa adds a dramatic colour and are personal favourites. Please see the chapter on Ingredients for how to make quinoa flour.

INGREDIENTS

150g (5oz) white or wholemeal spelt starter
   culture, ripe and at room temperature
400–425g (14–15oz) filtered water, at room
   temperature
100g (3½oz) quinoa flour

500g (17½oz) organic unbleached white spelt
   or high gluten (11–12 per cent) white
   premium bakers flour
2 teaspoons sea-salt, finely ground

METHOD

MEASURE INGREDIENTS (2–3 MINS): Use, preferably, a digital scale, to weigh all ingredients, including water. Put all ingredients in a non-metallic bowl, starting with water and starter, flour and the salt last.

MIX INGREDIENTS (2–3 MINS): Using a spatula or a wooden spoon, stir the ingredients together until they form a cohesive mass.

REST (15–20 MINS)

KNEADING (10–15 MINS): This non-sticky dough can be kneaded normally. Using the heel of your hand fold the dough onto itself, then do a quarter turn. Repeat the action of folding and turning until the dough becomes smooth and elastic. After you have done this for about 10-15 minutes, the dough will have developed some elasticity and it is smooth.

REST (20–30 MINS): This dough needs this 20–30 minute rest to allow the chestnut and kamut flour to absorb the water.

FIRST RISE (ABOUT 1 HOUR IN WARM WEATHER AND 2 HOURS IN COLD WEATHER): Leave the dough to rise in a covered container, at a comfortable room temperature, around 20–25°C (68–77°F).

TURNING/FOLDING: See 'Sourdough Bread Making Step-by-Step'. After turning/folding, let the dough sit for 10–15 minutes to relax the gluten.

DIVIDE AND SHAPE (5 MINS): Divide the dough into two and shape the loaves as desired. Mist the loaves with water.

SECOND/FINAL RISE (4–6 HOURS AT ROOM TEMPERATURE): Rise the shaped loaves until almost doubled at a comfortable room temperature, around 20–25°C (68–77°F), make sure the dough is covered, or mist frequently with water, to prevent drying.

PREHEAT YOUR OVEN TO 225°C (437°F)

BAKE: Bake for about 10 minutes, then reduce the oven to 205°C (400°F) for a further 20–25 minutes. If you are unsure whether the loaves have cooked through, turn the oven off, and let the loaves sit in the oven for a further 10 minutes. Remove loaves from oven, taking care not to burn yourself!

REST: Let the bread cool before cutting.

SUITABLE FOR FREEZING AND WILL KEEP FOR A COUPLE OF MONTHS FROZEN.

MALTED WHEAT OR MULTIGRAIN BREAD

MAKES 2 SMALL-TINNED LOAVES

Malted wheat gives this bread a delicious, burnt caramel aroma-it also adds a lot of fibre to this loaf. Half of the malted wheat is processed in a food processor to make malted wheat flour, the other half is left whole, to add crunch to the crumb. This bread also makes a delicious sandwich loaf. Note: If you cannot find (rolled) malted wheat, you can substitute it with rolled oats, rolled wheat or rolled spelt or you can use a mixture of rolled grains, which have been dry-roasted in a pan for about 7-10 minutes (until they start to caramelise).

INGREDIENTS

150g (5oz) white or wholemeal spelt culture, ripe and at room temperature
480–500g (1lb 1–1lb 2oz) filtered water, at room temperature
75g (2½oz) rolled malted wheat, ground into flour

75g (2½oz) rolled malted wheat, whole
400g (14oz) organic unbleached white wheat flour
250g (9oz) organic wholemeal wheat flour
3 teaspoons sea-salt, finely ground

METHOD

MEASURE INGREDIENTS (2–3 MINS): Use, preferably, a digital scale, to weigh all ingredients including water, put all ingredients in a non-metallic bowl, starting with water and starter, flours, excluding the whole malted wheat, and lastly the salt.

MIX INGREDIENTS (2–3 MINS): Using a spatula or a wooden spoon, stir the ingredients together until they form a cohesive mass.

REST (30 MINS): Rest the dough in the bowl for 30 minutes—this longer resting time is necessary for the ground malted wheat.

KNEADING – AIR KNEADING (5 MINS): Using your fingertips, throw your dough into the air and then slap/throw it onto your bench. After you have done this for about 5 minutes, the dough will have developed some elasticity. If your dough feels dry and hard, add some water by misting the water all around the dough, and let it absorb the water for 10–15 minutes before re-kneading, to incorporate the water.

REST (20-30 MINS): As a general rule, 20 minutes rest is sufficient, however, if your dough is still sticky, do a longer rise—this step allows the flour to absorb the water, giving the gluten a chance to realign itself. Your dough should feel soft and elastic, not hard and dry.

DO THE WINDOWPANE TEST: See 'Sourdough Bread Making Step-by-Step'.

FIRST RISE (ABOUT 1 HOUR IN WARM WEATHER AND 2 HOURS IN COLD WEATHER): Leave the dough to rise in a covered container, at a comfortable room temperature, around 20-25°C (68-77°F).

TURNING/FOLDING: See 'Sourdough Bread Making Step-by-Step'. After turning/folding, let the dough sit for 10–15 minutes to relax the gluten.

ADD THE WHOLE MALTED WHEAT: Add the whole malted wheat to the dough and knead lightly to distribute the seeds evenly.

DIVIDE AND SHAPE (5 MINS): Divide the dough into two equal portions and shape each portion into a tight ball, to fit into two small bread tins. Mist the loaves with water and sprinkle with extra rolled malted wheats.

SECOND/FINAL RISE (4-6 HOURS AT ROOM TEMPERATURE): Rise the shaped loaves until almost doubled at a comfortable room temperature, around 20–25°C (68–77°F), make sure the dough is covered, or mist frequently with water, to prevent drying.

PREHEAT YOUR OVEN TO 225°C (437°F)

BAKE: Bake for about 10 minutes, then reduce the oven to 205°C (400°F) for a further 25–35 minutes until cooked, depending on the size of your loaves. If you are unsure whether the loaves have cooked through, turn the oven off, and let the loaves sit in the oven for a further 10 minutes. Remove loaves from oven, taking care not to burn yourself!

REST: Let the bread cool before cutting.

SUITABLE FOR FREEZING AND WILL KEEP FOR A COUPLE OF MONTHS FROZEN.

Malted Wheat or
Multigrain bread

ENERGY LOAF

MAKES 1 SMALL- AND 1 MEDIUM-TINNED LOAVES OR 3 FREE-FORM LOAVES

This loaf is not as low GI as the rest of the High Protein/Low GI sourdough breads in this section as it includes some fresh dates, but I cannot resist including it, because it is one of the most delicious high protein and high fibre sourdough loaves I make. It is worth making the whole recipe, which will be enough for two or three loaves, one to eat fresh and one to freeze.

INGREDIENTS

SOAKER 1: START THIS THE DAY BEFORE MAKING THE DOUGH

150g (5oz) fresh dates, chopped roughly

50g (1¾oz) golden flaxseeds meal (or crushed flax seeds)

350g (12oz) water

Mix all above ingredients and let soak for 6-12 hours. This soaked mixture will keep in the fridge for up to three days.

SOAKER 2: START THIS THE DAY BEFORE MAKING THE DOUGH

30g (1oz) oat bran

100g (3½oz) thick yoghurt, full cream

Mix all above ingredients and let soak for 6-12 hours. This soaked mixture will keep in the fridge for up to three days.

Soaked mixtures 1 and 2
250g (9oz) wholemeal spelt culture, ripe and at room temperature
200g (7oz) sunflower seeds, ground into flour
500g (17½oz) wholemeal wheat or spelt

50g (1¾oz) poppy seed or sesame seeds
2 teaspoons sea-salt, finely ground
50g (1¾oz) raw organic sugar, or 4 teaspoons honey or 2 teaspoons agave nectar

METHOD

MEASURE INGREDIENTS (2–3 MINS): Use, preferably, a digital scale, to weigh the ingredients. Place all the remaining ingredients into a large bowl, including the two soaked mixtures.

MIX INGREDIENTS (5 MINS): Using a spatula or a wooden spoon, stir the ingredients together until they form a cohesive mass.

REST (15–20 MINS)

KNEADING (10 MINS): Using the heel of your hand, gently knead the dough for 2–3 minutes. The dough will be quite tacky to start off with but after you have done this for about 5 minutes, the dough will have developed some elasticity. Knead until all the ingredients are evenly distributed and mixed into the dough. The finished dough should feel elastic, soft and slightly sticky. If your dough feels dry and hard, add some water by misting the water all around the dough, and let it absorb the water for 10-15 minutes before re-kneading, to incorporate the water.

DIVIDE AND SHAPE (5 MINS): Divide and shape the dough into two or three—shape loaves as desired.Mist the loaf/loaves with water and sprinkle with extra seeds if desired.

SECOND/FINAL RISE (4-6 HOURS AT ROOM TEMPERATURE): Rise the loaves until almost doubled at a comfortable room temperature, around 20–25°C (68–77°F). Make sure the dough is covered, or mist frequently with water, to prevent drying.

PREHEAT YOUR OVEN TO 215°C (420°F)

BAKE: Bake for about 10 minutes, then reduce the oven to 175°C (349°F) for a further 25–35 minutes until cooked, depending on the size of your loaves. The loaves should be dark brown in colour, not golden brown. Turn the oven off, and let the loaves sit in the oven for a further 10 minutes. Remove loaves from oven, taking care not to burn yourself!

REST: Let the bread cool before cutting.

SUITABLE FOR FREEZING AND WILL KEEP FOR A COUPLE OF MONTHS FROZEN.

Energy Loaf

Almond Spelt Loaf

ALMOND SPELT LOAF

This loaf will fill your house with a truly delicious aroma! Almond adds both a nutty aroma and a delicious crunch to this bread. To jazz it up, I also add vanilla bean paste. Vanilla complements the gorgeous aroma of almond and gives the illusion of sweetness without adding any sugar. For freshness, I prefer to grind my own almonds to make almond meal. Egg whites add extra protein and give the loaf a higher volume.

INGREDIENTS

150g (5oz) white or wholemeal spelt culture, ripe and at room temperature

450g (15½oz) filtered water, at room temperature

50g (1¾oz) egg whites

125g (4oz) almond meal

475g (16oz) organic unbleached white spelt

2 teaspoons sea-salt, finely ground

1 teaspoon vanilla bean extract, optional

ALMOND MIXTURE:

75–100g (2½–3 ½oz) almonds, chopped roughly, leave some for topping

METHOD

MEASURE INGREDIENTS (2–3 MINS): Use, preferably, a digital scale, to weigh all ingredients, including water. Put all ingredients in a non-metallic bowl, starting with water and starter, flour, including almond meal, and lastly the salt.

MIX INGREDIENTS (2–3 MINS): Using a spatula or a wooden spoon, stir the ingredients together until they form a cohesive mass.

REST (30 MINS)

KNEADING – AIR KNEADING (5 MINS): Using your fingertips, throw your dough into the air and then slap/throw it onto your bench. After you have done this for about 5 minutes, the dough will have developed some elasticity. If your dough feels dry and hard, add some water by misting the water all around the dough, and let it absorb the water for 10–15 minutes before re-kneading to incorporate the water.

REST (20-30 MINS): Your dough should feel soft and elastic, not hard and dry.

FIRST RISE (ABOUT 1 HOUR IN WARM WEATHER AND 2 HOURS IN COLD WEATHER): Leave the dough to rise in a covered container, at a comfortable room temperature, around 20-25°C (68-77°F).

TURNING/FOLDING: See 'Sourdough Bread Making Step-by-Step'. After turning/folding, let the dough sit for 10-15 minutes to relax the gluten.

ADD: Add the chopped almonds to the dough and knead lightly to distribute the seeds evenly. Leave some chopped almonds to sprinkle on top of the dough, after dividing and shaping.

DIVIDE AND SHAPE (5 MINS): You can either make one medium-sized loaf or two small ones. Divide and shape the loaves as desired. Mist the loaf/loaves with water and sprinkle with extra chopped almonds, if desired.

SECOND/FINAL RISE (4–6 HOURS AT ROOM TEMPERATURE): Rise the shaped loaf/loaves until almost doubled at a comfortable room temperature around 20–25°C (68–77°F). Make sure the dough is covered, or mist with water frequently, to prevent drying.

PREHEAT YOUR OVEN TO 205°C (400°F)

BAKE: Bake for about 10 minutes, then reduce the oven to 205°C (400°F) for a further 25–35 minutes until cooked, depending on the size of your loaf/loaves. If you are unsure whether the loaves have cooked through, turn the oven off, and let the loaves sit in the oven for a further 10 minutes. Remove loaves from oven, taking care not to burn yourself!

REST: Let the bread cool before cutting.

SUITABLE FOR FREEZING AND WILL KEEP FOR A COUPLE OF MONTHS FROZEN.

Multi-purpose Soft Sourdough Rolls with Chocolate Ganache

SOFT
SOURDOUGH

MULTI-PURPOSE SOFT SOURDOUGH ROLLS

MAKES ABOUT 20-24 ROLLS/BUNS OR 2 SMALL-TINNED LOAVES

This is the nicest and most basic 'soft' sourdough bread-you can make it into rolls or loaves. You will make these soft rolls over and over again. This bread also freezes well. You can use this recipe to make chocolate, cheese or even seasoned meat or vegetable filled rolls. I have used this recipe to make ham and cheese 'faux' croissants. Sprinkling each roll with aromatic sesame or poppy seeds will transform the taste of these to another level of yumminess! You can add vanilla bean paste if you want to fill these rolls with chocolate ganache.

INGREDIENTS

150g (5oz) active white wheat or spelt sourdough starter
400g (14oz) full cream organic yoghurt (straight from the fridge or at room temperature in winter time)

200–225g (7–8oz) filtered water
900g (36oz) white spelt or wheat flour
4 teaspoons sea salt
Sesame seeds or poppy seeds for sprinkling

METHOD

MEASURE INGREDIENTS (2–3MINS): Use, preferably, a digital scale, to weigh all ingredients, then put all ingredients in a non-metallic bowl, starting with water, starter and yoghurt, then the rest of the ingredients and lastly the salt.

MIX INGREDIENTS (2–3 MINS): Using a spatula or a wooden spoon, stir the ingredients together until they form a cohesive mass.

REST (20 MINS): This step is most important for doughs containing wholegrain/wholemeal flour, as it allows a greater absorption of water.

KNEADING – AIR KNEADING (15–20 MINS): Using your fingertips, throw your dough into the air and then slap/throw it onto your bench. After you have done this for about 5 minutes, you will start to feel a slight elasticity. This is a soft, rather than elastic, dough but you will develop more elasticity if you continue to knead for an extra 10-15 minutes. You may find it easier to oil your bench and your hands.

REST (20–30 MINS): This dough will develop some elasticity, but is mostly a soft, slightly sticky dough.

ADJUST FLOUR OR WATER (IF NECESSARY): If after the 30 minutes rest period your dough still feels wet or too dry, then this is the time to add more water or flour.

FINAL KNEADING (5 MINS ONLY IF YOU ARE ADJUSTING FLOUR/WATER)

DO THE WINDOWPANE TEST: See 'Sourdough Bread Making Step-by-Step'.

FIRST RISE (2 HOURS): Gather your dough together and shape into a ball. Let it rest in a non-metallic container or a bowl, covered with a wet tea towel or wet cling wrap. Let your dough rise to about one and a quarter times its size—the time taken will vary.

DOUGH RETARDATION (OPTIONAL, OVERNIGHT): Cover the dough and leave it in the fridge, overnight. The next day, take the dough out of the fridge and leave to thaw for about an hour.

TURNING/FOLDING: See 'Sourdough Bread Making Step-by-Step'. After turning/folding, let the dough sit for 10–15 minutes to relax the gluten.

DIVIDE AND SHAPE (5 MINS): Divide and shape the dough as desired. Brush the top of the dough with milk if you wish. Milk will create a soft crust. Sprinkle with seeds, if you wish.

SECOND/FINAL RISE (ABOUT 4–8 HOURS): Rise again until almost doubled, at a comfortable room temperature around 20–25°C (68–77°F), make sure the dough is covered or mist with water to prevent drying. Do the indentation test.

PREHEAT YOUR OVEN TO 225°C (437°F)

BAKE: Bake for about 10 minutes, then reduce the oven to 180°C (350°F) for a further 20-25 minutes for tinned loaves or 10–15 minutes for buns/rolls until browned and cooked, depending on size and shape of the dough. If you are unsure whether the loaves have cooked through, turn the oven off, and let the loaves sit in the oven for a further 10 minutes. Remove loaves from oven, taking care not to burn yourself!

REST: Let the bread cool before cutting.

SUITABLE FOR FREEZING AND WILL KEEP FOR A COUPLE OF MONTHS FROZEN.

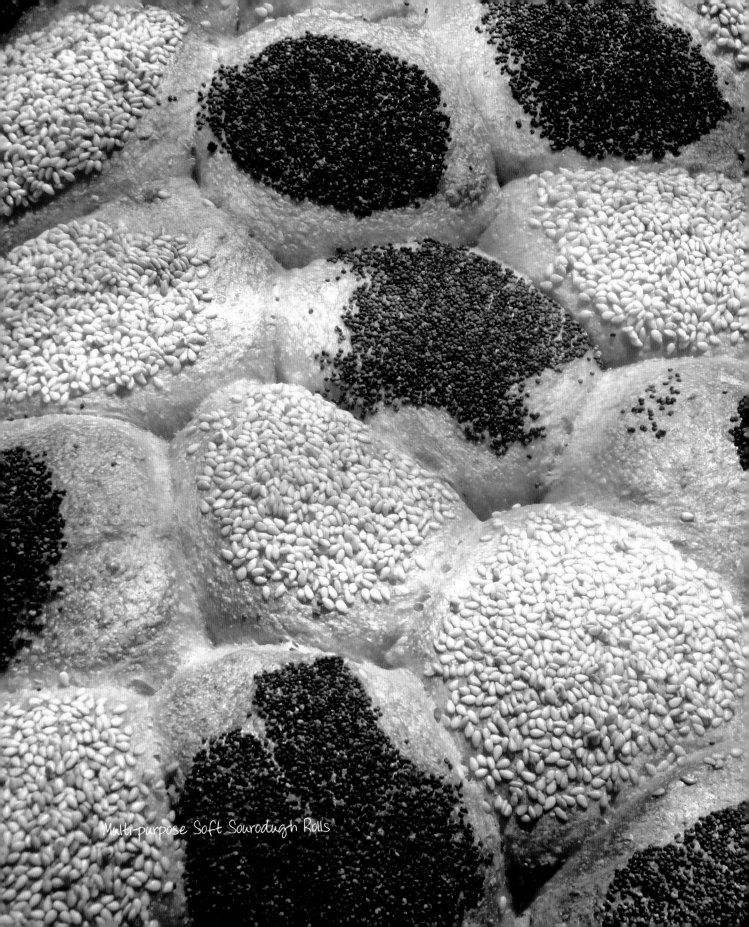
Multi-purpose Soft Sourdough Rolls

Eggless Brioche Loaf.

EGGLESS BRIOCHE LOAF

MAKES 2 SMALL-TINNED LOAVES

One of my fondest childhood memories was a trip to a coffee plantation, located on a mountain town about 2 hours away from my hometown in Solo, Indonesia. My family and I always visited a little Dutch bakery nearby, where they made the most amazing bread, pastries and cake. My favourite was a brioche-like loaf which was sprinkled with sugar crystals.

INGREDIENTS

150g (5oz) active white wheat or spelt sourdough starter
300g (10½oz) full cream organic yoghurt (straight from the fridge or at room temperature in winter time)
225g (8oz) freshly squeezed orange juice

900g (32oz) white wheat or spelt flour
50g (1¾oz) agave syrup, honey or maple syrup
100g (3½oz) butter, softened
25g (¾oz) coffee sugar crystals for sprinkling
1 tablespoon sea-salt

METHOD

MEASURE INGREDIENTS (2–3 MINS): Use, preferably, a digital scale, to weigh all ingredients. Then put all ingredients, except butter and sugar crystals, in a non-metallic bowl, starting with starter and yoghurt, then the rest of the ingredients and lastly the salt.

MIX INGREDIENTS (2–3 MINS): Using a spatula or a wooden spoon, stir the ingredients together until they form a cohesive mass.

REST (15–20 MINS)

KNEADING – AIR KNEADING (20–25 MINS): Using your fingertips, throw your dough into the air and then slap/throw it onto your bench. After you have done this for about 10 minutes, the dough will have developed some elasticity. Knead in softened butter. Continue kneading for another 10–15 minutes until your dough is elastic. This long kneading is to develop a fine crumb in your brioche. This is a soft, rather than an elastic, dough, but you will develop elasticity if you continue to knead that extra 10–15 minutes. You may find it easier to lightly oil your bench and your hands.

REST (20–30 MINS): Your dough should feel soft, elastic and slightly sticky.

DO THE WINDOWPANE TEST: See 'Sourdough Bread Making Step-by-Step'.

FIRST RISE (2 HOURS): Gather your dough together and shape into a ball. Let it rest in a non-metallic container or a bowl covered with a wet tea-towel or wet cling wrap. Let your dough rise to about one and a quarter times its size—the time taken will vary.

DOUGH RETARDATION (OPTIONAL, OVERNIGHT): Cover the dough and leave the dough in the fridge, overnight. The next day, take the dough out of the fridge and leave to thaw for about an hour.

TURNING/FOLDING: See 'Sourdough Bread Making Step-by-Step'. After turning/folding, let the dough sit for 10–15 minutes to relax the gluten.

DIVIDE AND SHAPE (5 MINS): Divide and shape the dough as desired. Brush the top of the dough with milk if you wish. Milk will create a soft crust. Sprinkle with coffee sugar crystals, if desired.

SECOND/FINAL RISE (ABOUT 4–8 HOURS): Rise again until almost doubled, at a comfortable room temperature around 20–25°C (68–77°F). Make sure the dough is covered or mist with water to prevent drying. Do the indentation test.

PREHEAT YOUR OVEN TO 225°C (437°F).

BAKE: Bake for about 10 minutes, then reduce the oven to 180°C (350°F) for a further 25–30 minutes for tinned loaves. If you are unsure whether the loaves have cooked through, turn the oven off, and let the loaves sit in the oven for a further 10 minutes. Remove loaves from oven, taking care not to burn yourself!

REST: Let the bread cool before cutting.

SUITABLE FOR FREEZING AND WILL KEEP FOR A COUPLE OF MONTHS FROZEN.

SOFT HERB ROLLS

MAKES ABOUT 12-14 ROLLS/PULL-APART BUNS

This recipe will give really soft rolls with a 'peel-able' crumb, almost like the crumb of commercially-made yeasted bread. The small amount of olive oil will make these rolls soft for a few days. It is best to refresh/warm them before serving. A bowl of hot pumpkin soup marries well with these rolls.

INGREDIENTS

100g (3½oz) active white wheat or spelt
    sourdough starter
275g (9½oz) full cream organic yoghurt
    (straight from the fridge or at room
    temperature in winter time)
150g (5oz) filtered water

700g (24oz) white spelt or wheat flour
50g (1¾oz) extra virgin olive oil
2 teaspoons sea-salt
2–3 teaspoons dried Greek oregano or dried
    mixed herbs of your choice

METHOD

MEASURE INGREDIENTS (2–3MINS): Use, preferably, a digital scale, to weigh all ingredients, then put all ingredients, except the herbs in a non-metallic bowl, starting with water, starter and yoghurt, then the rest of the ingredients and lastly, salt.

MIX INGREDIENTS (2–3 MINS): Using a spatula or a wooden spoon, stir the ingredients together until they form a cohesive mass.

REST (20 MINS): Rest the dough in the bowl for 20 minutes.

KNEADING – AIR KNEADING (15–20 MINS): Using your fingertips, throw your dough into the air and then slap/throw it onto your bench. After you have done this for about 5 minutes, the dough will have developed some elasticity. This is a soft, rather than an elastic, dough, but you will develop elasticity if you continue to knead for an extra 10–15 minutes. You may find it easier to lightly oil your bench and your hands.

REST (20–30 MINS): This dough will develop some elasticity, but is mostly a soft, slightly sticky dough.

DO THE WINDOWPANE TEST: See 'Sourdough Bread Making Step-by-Step'.

ADD: Add the herbs and knead well to distribute the herbs evenly throughout the dough.

FIRST RISE (2 HOURS): Gather your dough together and shape into a ball. Let it rest in a non-metallic container or a bowl covered with a wet tea-towel or wet cling wrap. Let your dough rises to about one and a quarter times its size—the time taken will vary.

DOUGH RETARDATION (OPTIONAL, OVERNIGHT): Cover the dough and leave the dough in the fridge, overnight. The next day, take the dough out of the fridge and leave to thaw for about an hour.

TURNING/FOLDING: See 'Sourdough Bread Making Step-by-Step'. After turning/folding, let the dough sit for 10-15 minutes to relax the gluten.

DIVIDE AND SHAPE (5 MINS): Divide and shape the dough into 80–90g (2 ½–3oz) pieces—no larger as your buns will not cook through. Then round each dough piece into a tight ball. Place each individual ball onto a square piece of baking paper. Alternatively, to make pull-apart buns, snuggle these buns together in a deep roasting pan or lamington pan. Brush the top of the dough with milk if you wish. Milk will create a soft crust. Sprinkle with herbs.

SECOND/FINAL RISE ABOUT (4–8 HOURS): Rise again until almost doubled, at a comfortable room temperature, around 20–25°C (68–77°F), make sure the dough is covered or mist with water to prevent drying. Do the indentation test.

PREHEAT YOUR OVEN TO 225°C (437°F)

BAKE: Bake for about 10 minutes, then reduce the oven to 180°C (350°F) 10–15 minutes for single buns/rolls or 20–25 minutes for pull-apart buns, until browned and cooked. Remove buns/rolls from oven, taking care not to burn yourself! Brush with melted butter and cover with a tea towel to keep the buns/rolls soft.

SUITABLE FOR FREEZING AND WILL KEEP FOR A COUPLE OF MONTHS FROZEN.

Soft Herb Rolls

Basil Tomato Parmesan Loaf

BASIL TOMATO PARMESAN LOAF

MAKES 3 FREE-FORM LOAVES OR 3 FOCCACIAS

An abundance of basil in my garden this summer has prompted me to sneak basil into all sorts of things. This recipe combines all that I love in my summer veggie patch-basil and tomatoes.

INGREDIENTS

200g (7oz) active white wheat/spelt
  sourdough starter
125g (4oz) mascarpone, quark or any cream
  cheese of your choice
480 (17oz) filtered water
850g (30oz) white wheat/spelt flour

2 teaspoons sea salt
25g (¾oz) basil leaves, chopped
75g (2½oz) semi-dried tomatoes
50–75g (1¾–2 ½oz) parmesan cheese and
extra 25g (¾oz) for sprinkling

METHOD

MEASURE INGREDIENTS (2–3 MINS): Use, preferably a digital scale, to weigh all ingredients. Put all 'dough' ingredients in a non-metallic bowl, starting with water, starter and cream cheese then the rest of the ingredients and lastly, salt. Do not include basil leaves, semi dried tomatoes and parmesan cheese at this stage.

MIX INGREDIENTS (2–3 MINS): Using a spatula or a wooden spoon, stir the ingredients together until they form a cohesive mass.

REST (20 MINS)

KNEADING – AIR KNEADING (15 MINS): Using your fingertips, throw your dough into the air and then slap/throw it onto your bench. After you have done this for about 5 minutes, the dough will have developed some elasticity. This is a soft, rather than elastic, dough, but you will develop elasticity if you continue to knead for an extra 10 minutes. You may find it easier to lightly oil your bench and your hands.

REST (20–30 MINS): Your dough should feel soft, elastic and slightly sticky.

ADJUST FLOUR OR WATER (IF NECESSARY): If after the 30 minute rest period your dough still feels wet or too dry, then this is the time to add more water or flour.

FINAL KNEADING (5 MINS ONLY IF YOU ARE ADJUSTING FLOUR/WATER)

DO THE WINDOWPANE TEST: See 'Sourdough Bread Making Step-by-Step'.

FIRST RISE (2 HOURS): Gather your dough together and shape into a ball. Let it rest in a non-metallic container or a bowl covered with a wet tea towel or wet cling wrap. Let your dough rise to about one and a quarter times its size—the time taken will vary.

DOUGH RETARDATION (OPTIONAL, OVERNIGHT): Cover the dough and leave the dough in the fridge overnight. The next day, take the dough out of the fridge and leave to thaw for about an hour.

TURNING/FOLDING: See 'Sourdough Bread Making Step-by-Step'. After turning/folding, let the dough sit for 10–15 minutes to relax the gluten.

ADD (5 MINS): Add chopped basil leaves, semi-dried tomatoes and parmesan. Knead well to distribute these ingredients evenly throughout the dough.

DIVIDE AND SHAPE (5 MINS): Divide and shape the dough as desired. Mist the top of the dough with water and sprinkle with extra parmesan.

SECOND/FINAL RISE (ABOUT 4–8 HOURS): Rise again until almost doubled, at a comfortable room temperature, around 20–25°C (68-77°F), make sure the dough is covered or mist with water to prevent drying. Do the indentation test.

PREHEAT YOUR OVEN TO 225°C (437°F)

BAKE: Bake for about 10 minutes, then reduce the oven to 185°C (165°F) for a further 20–25 minutes until loaves are browned and cooked, depending on size and shape of the dough. If you are unsure whether the loaves have cooked through, turn the oven off, and let the loaves sit in the oven for a further 10 minutes. Remove loaves from oven, taking care not to burn yourself!

REST: Let the bread cool before cutting.

SUITABLE FOR FREEZING AND WILL KEEP FOR A COUPLE OF MONTHS FROZEN.

MUSHROOM & THYME LOAF

MAKES 2 TO 3 FREE-FORM LOAVES

I am actually quite baffled as to how I have never come across bread flavoured with mushroom! So here is my delicious aromatic sourdough version. I could not find any exotic mushrooms here in Perth in the middle of summer, so I used Portobello mushrooms. For those of you who have access to more exotic varieties of mushrooms, feel free to experiment. This is a great bread to serve with a bowl of homemade soup.

INGREDIENTS

STEP 1

200g (7oz) Portobello mushrooms
few sprigs thyme

1 tablespoon extra virgin olive oil

Chop up Portobello mushrooms. In a pan, sauté mushrooms, thyme and oil for 10 minutes. Take off heat and drain, reserving the mushroom water. Let the mushrooms cool.

150g (5oz) wholemeal spelt culture, ripe and
    at room temperature
All of the mushroom water, plus more water
    to make up 450g total water required.
680g (24oz) organic unbleached white wheat
    or spelt flour

200g (7oz) wholemeal spelt flour
250–300g (9–10½oz) portobello mushrooms,
    process into a paste
60ml (2fl oz) organic soy sauce or tamari
1 teaspoon sea-salt, finely ground

METHOD

MEASURE INGREDIENTS (2–3 MINS): Use, preferably, a digital scale, to weigh all ingredients in a non-metallic bowl. Put in all ingredients, except the cooked mushrooms, starting with liquids, flour and lastly the salt.

MIX INGREDIENTS (2–3 MINS): Using a spatula or a wooden spoon, stir the ingredients together until they form a cohesive mass.

REST (15–20 MINS)

KNEADING – AIR KNEADING (10–15 MINS): Using your fingertips, throw your dough into the air and then slap/throw it onto your bench. After you have done this for about 5 minutes, the dough will have developed some elasticity. Knead some more until the dough develops into a soft and an elastic dough.

REST (20–30 MINS): Your dough should feel soft, elastic and slightly sticky.

DO THE WINDOW PANE TEST: See 'Sourdough Bread Making Step-by-Step'.

ADD (5 MINS): Add and knead in all of the cooled sautéed mushrooms until they are well distributed throughout the dough.

FIRST RISE (ABOUT 1 HOUR IN WARM WEATHER AND 2 HOURS IN COLD WEATHER): Gather the dough into a ball and leave the dough to rise in a covered container, at a comfortable room temperature around 20–25°C (68–77°F).

TURNING/FOLDING: See 'Sourdough Bread Making Step-by-Step'. After turning/folding, let the dough sit for 10–15 minutes to relax the gluten.

DIVIDE AND SHAPE (5 MINS): Divide the dough into 2–3 pieces. Flatten each piece into a rough rectanglar shape. Distribute evenly half of the mushrooms on top of the dough. Roll tightly and tuck in at the sides. Mist the loaves with water and sprinkle with some chopped mushrooms, if desired.

SECOND/FINAL RISE (4–6 HOURS AT ROOM TEMPERATURE): Rise the shaped loaves until almost doubled, about 4–6 hours at a comfortable room temperature around 20–25°C (68–77°F). Make sure the dough is covered or mist with water frequently to prevent drying.

PREHEAT YOUR OVEN TO 225°C (437°F)

BAKE: Bake for about 8–10 minutes, then reduce the oven to 215°C (419°F) for a further 20–30 minutes, depending on the size of the loaves. If you are unsure whether the loaves have cooked through, turn the oven off, and let the loaves sit in the oven for a further 10 minutes. Remove loaves from oven, taking care not to burn yourself!

REST: Let the bread cool before cutting.

SUITABLE FOR FREEZING AND WILL KEEP FOR A COUPLE OF MONTHS FROZEN.

Mushroom & Thyme Loaf

Roasted Peppers, Semi-dried Tomatoes 'n' Cheese Scrolls

ROASTED PEPPERS, SEMI-DRIED TOMATOES 'N' CHEESE SCROLLS

MAKES ABOUT 8-10 SCROLLS

These cheese scrolls are the essence of summer. They are perfect for an afternoon tea party. For vegemite/marmite lovers, you can use this dough to make your favourite cheesy-mite scrolls.

INGREDIENTS

100g (3 ½oz) active white wheat or spelt
   sourdough starter
250g (9oz) full cream organic yoghurt
   (straight from the fridge or at room
   temperature in winter time)
200g (7oz) filtered water
500g (17½oz) white spelt or wheat flour

2 teaspoons sea-salt

FILLINGS
125g (4oz) roasted peppers
125g (4oz) semi-dried tomatoes
150g (5oz) cheddar cheese or gruyere
1 ½ teaspoons dried oregano

METHOD

MEASURE INGREDIENTS (2–3 MINS): Use, preferably, a digital scale, to weigh all ingredients. Put all ingredients in a non-metallic bowl, starting with water, starter and yoghurt, then the rest of the ingredients and lastly, salt.

MIX INGREDIENTS (2–3 MINS): Using a spatula or a wooden spoon, stir the ingredients together until they form a cohesive mass.

REST (20 MINS): Rest the dough in the bowl for 20 minutes.

KNEADING – AIR KNEADING (15–20 MINS): Using your fingertips, throw your dough into the air and then slap/throw it onto your bench. After you have done this for about 5 minutes, the dough will have developed some elasticity. This is a soft, rather than elastic, dough, but you will develop elasticity if you continue to knead for an extra 10–15 minutes. You may find it easier to oil your bench and your hands.

REST (20–30 MINS): Your dough should feel soft, elastic and slightly sticky.

ADJUST FLOUR OR WATER (IF NECESSARY): If after the 30 minute rest period your dough still feels wet or too dry, then this is the time to add more water or flour.

FINAL KNEADING (5 MINS ONLY IF YOU ARE ADJUSTING FLOUR/WATER)

DO THE WINDOWPANE TEST: See 'Sourdough Bread Making Step-by-Step'.

FIRST RISE (2 HOURS): Gather your dough together and try to make a ball. Let it rest in a non-metallic container or a bowl covered with a wet tea towel or a wet cling wrap. Let your dough rises to about one and a quarter times its size—the time taken will vary.

DOUGH RETARDATION (OPTIONAL, OVERNIGHT) Cover the dough and leave the dough in the fridge, overnight. The next day, take the dough out of the fridge and leave to thaw for about an hour.

TURNING/FOLDING: After turning/folding, let the dough sit for 10-15 minutes to relax the gluten. See 'Sourdough Bread Making Step-by-Step'.

DIVIDE AND SHAPE (5 MINS): Roll the dough into a rectangle of 30 x 40cm (12 x 16ins), on a lightly floured surface. Distribute the toppings of roasted peppers, semi-dried tomatoes, cheese and sprinkle the oregano. Make sure the filling is evenly distributed over the entire dough. Using a rolling pin, lightly roll over the dough to press in the filling. Roll up the rectangle into a tight 40cm (16ins) long log. Wrap log in plastic and freeze for about 45 minutes until reasonably firm, so that it is easy to cut. Cut the log into 12 pieces, depending on how thick you like your scrolls. Lay the slices spiral side down, snuggling each other in a deep roasting/lamington pan (24 x 34cm (9.6 x 13.6ins) and 5–6cm (2–2½oz) deep).

SECOND/FINAL RISE (4-6 HOURS AT ROOM TEMPERATURE): Rise the scrolls until almost doubled, at a comfortable room temperature, around 20–25°C (68–77°F). Make sure the dough is covered, or mist frequently with water, to prevent drying.

PREHEAT YOUR OVEN TO 200ºC (400ºF)

BAKE: Bake for about 10 minutes, then reduce the oven to 180°C (350°F) for a further 15–20 minutes. If you are unsure whether the scrolls have cooked through, turn the oven off, and let the loaves sit in the oven for a further 5 minutes.Remove pans from oven, and immediately invert the scrolls onto a cooling rack. Turn the scrolls the right way up. Enjoy.

OLIVE OIL & MILK FOCACCIA

This is one of those breads you will enjoy eating and kneading and it will soon be one of your favourite sourdoughs. The dough is soft and elastic, made possible by the exclusive use of buttermilk in the dough. It will also taste beautiful toasted. If you like, you can add olives or sundried tomatoes into this dough. It also makes a nice replacement for Turkish bread for making sandwiches.

INGREDIENTS

300g (10½oz) white wheat or spelt starter culture, ripe and at room temperature
450g (15oz) buttermilk at room temperature
50–75g (1¾–2 ½oz) olive oil

900g (32oz) organic unbleached white wheat or spelt flour
3 teaspoons sea-salt, finely ground
50g (1¾oz) raw organic sugar (optional)

METHOD

MEASURE INGREDIENTS (2–3 MINS): Use, preferably, a digital scale, to weigh all ingredients, including water. Put all ingredients in a non-metallic bowl, starting with water and starter, flour, sugar and lastly the salt.

MIX INGREDIENTS (2–3 MINS): Using a spatula or a wooden spoon, stir the ingredients together until they form a cohesive mass.

REST (15–20 MINS)

KNEADING – AIR KNEADING (15 MINS):
Using your fingertips, throw your dough into the air and then slap/throw it onto your bench. After you have done this for about 5 minutes, the dough will have developed some elasticity. Knead another 10 minutes, to create a soft and an elastic dough. The dough should also be slightly sticky.

REST (20-30 MINS): Your dough should feel soft, elastic and slightly sticky.

DO THE WINDOW PANE TEST: See 'Sourdough Bread Making Step-by-Step'.

FIRST RISE (2 HOURS): Gather your dough together and shape into a ball. Let it rest in a covered non-metallic container or a bowl covered with a wet tea-towel or a wet cling wrap. Let your dough rises to about one and a quarter times its size—the time taken will vary.

DOUGH RETARDATION (OPTIONAL, OVERNIGHT): Cover the dough and leave the dough overnight in the fridge. The next day take the dough out of the fridge and leave to thaw for about an hour.

TURNING/FOLDING: See 'Sourdough Bread Making Step-by-Step'. After turning/folding, let the dough sit for 10–15 minutes to relax the gluten.

DIVIDE AND SHAPE (5 MINS): Divide the dough into two or three equal pieces and stretch or roll the dough to about 2cm (¾in) thick, pockmark the dough with your fingers. Place each individual focaccia onto a square piece of baking paper. Brush the surface of the focaccia with milk.

SECOND/FINAL RISE (ABOUT 4–8 HOURS): Rise again until almost doubled, at a comfortable room temperature, around 20–25°C (68–77°F). Make sure the dough is covered or mist with water to prevent drying. Do the indentation test.

PREHEAT YOUR OVEN TO 235°C (450°F)

BAKE: Bake for about 10 minutes, then reduce the oven to 200°C (400°F) 10–15 minutes, until browned and cooked. Remove focaccia from oven, taking care not to burn yourself! Enjoy while warm!

SUITABLE FOR FREEZING AND WILL KEEP FOR A COUPLE OF MONTHS FROZEN.

Olive Oil & Milk Focaccia

Focaccia Con L'Uva

FOCACCIA CON L'UVA

MAKES 2-3 FOCACCIA, DEPENDING ON SIZE

This focaccia with caramelised grapes on top looks really impressive on any table! It is remarkably easy to make, all you need is a soft focaccia dough and some sweet grapes (green or red, your choice).

INGREDIENTS

100g (3½oz) active white wheat or spelt
    sourdough starter
275g (9½oz) full cream organic yoghurt
    (straight from the fridge or at room
    temperature in winter time)
150g (5oz) filtered water
700g (24oz) white spelt or wheat flour

50g (1¾oz) extra virgin olive oil
2 teaspoons sea-salt

TOPPINGS

500g (17½oz) sweet red or green grapes
150g (5oz) demerara sugar or organic raw sugar

METHOD

MEASURE INGREDIENTS (2–3 MINS): Use, preferably, a digital scale, to weigh all ingredients. Then put all 'dough' ingredients in a non-metallic bowl, starting with water, starter and yoghurt, then the rest of the ingredients and lastly the salt.

MIX INGREDIENTS (2-3 MINS): Using a spatula or a wooden spoon, stir the ingredients together until they form a cohesive mass.

REST (20 MINS)

KNEADING – AIR KNEADING (10–15 MINS): Using your fingertips, throw your dough into the air and then slap/throw it onto your bench. After you have done this for about 5 minutes, the dough will have developed some elasticity. This is a soft, rather than elastic, dough, but you will develop elasticity if you continue to knead for an extra 10 minutes. You may find it easier to oil your bench and your hands.

REST (20–30 MINS): Your dough should feel soft, elastic and slightly sticky.

DO THE WINDOWPANE TEST: See 'Sourdough Bread Making Step-by-Step'.

FIRST RISE (2 HOURS): Gather your dough together and shape into a ball, let it rest in a non-metallic container or a bowl covered with a wet tea-towel or a wet cling wrap. Let your dough rises to about one and a quarter times its size—the time taken will vary.

DOUGH RETARDATION (OPTIONAL, OVERNIGHT): Cover the dough and leave the dough overnight in the fridge. The next day take the dough out of the fridge and leave to thaw for about an hour.

TURNING/FOLDING: See 'Sourdough Bread Making Step-by-Step'. After turning/folding, let the dough sit for 10–15 minutes to relax the gluten.

DIVIDE AND SHAPE (5 MINS): Divide the dough into two or three equal pieces and stretch or roll the dough to about 2cm (0.8in) thick, pockmark the dough with your fingers. Place each individual focaccia onto a square piece of baking paper. Brush the surface of the focaccia with water. Sprinkle the sugar on top of the focaccia, then pull apart the whole grapes and distribute all over the surface of the focaccia. Sprinkle more of the sugar on top of the grapes.

SECOND/FINAL RISE ABOUT (4–8 HOURS): Rise again until almost doubled, at a comfortable room temperature, around 20-25°C (68-77°F), make sure the dough is covered or mist with water to prevent drying. Do the indentation test.

PREHEAT YOUR OVEN TO 235°C (455°F)

BAKE: Bake for about 10 minutes, then reduce the oven to 200°C (400°F) for 15–20 minutes, until browned and cooked and the grapes have burst and caramelised. Remove focaccia from oven, taking care not to burn yourself! Enjoy while warm.

Sticky Pecan Scrolls

SWEET
INDULGENCES

STICKY PECAN SCROLLS

MAKES 10-12 SCROLLS

Who can resist the sweet caramel aroma of freshly baked sticky pecan scrolls? You will find this sourdough version as light and delightful as the commercially yeasted one, and it is better for you as long as you don't over-indulge!

INGREDIENTS

DOUGH

200g (7oz) active white starter culture
300g (10½oz) full cream yoghurt
60g (2oz) egg yolk or whole eggs
600g (21oz) organic white baker's flour (or white spelt)
50g (1¾oz) raw organic sugar
1 teaspoon vanilla bean paste
2 teaspoons seasalt

THE FILLING

350g (12oz) raw organic sugar
50g (1¾oz) organic salted butter
½ heaped teaspoon of cinnamon
200g (7oz) chopped pecans

TOPPING

100g (3½ oz) whole pecans
200g (7oz) butter
400g (14oz) raw organic sugar

METHOD

MEASURE INGREDIENTS (2–3 MINS): Use, preferably, a digital scale, to weigh all dough ingredients. Put all dough ingredients in a non-metallic bowl, starting with all of the liquids, flour and lastly the salt.

MIX INGREDIENTS (2–3 MINS): Using a spatula or a wooden spoon, stir the ingredients together until they form a cohesive mass.

REST (15-20 MINS)

KNEADING – AIR KNEADING (5 MINS): Using your fingertips, throw your dough into the air and then slap/throw it onto your bench. After you have done this for about 5 minutes, the dough will have developed some elasticity.

REST (20–30 MINS): Your dough should feel soft, elastic and slightly sticky.

DO THE WINDOWPANE TEST: See 'Sourdough Bread Making Step-by-Step'.

FIRST RISE (ABOUT 1 HOUR IN WARM WEATHER AND 2 HOURS IN COLD WEATHER): Leave the dough to rise in a covered container, at a comfortable room temperature, around 20–25°C (68–77°F).

DOUGH RETARDATION (OPTIONAL, OVERNIGHT): Cover the dough and leave the dough in the fridge, overnight. The next day, take the dough out of the fridge and leave to thaw for about an hour.

TURNING/FOLDING: See 'Sourdough Bread Making Step-by-Step'. After turning/folding, let the dough sit for 10–15 minutes to relax the gluten.

DIVIDE AND SHAPE: Blitz all of the filling ingredients, except pecans, in a food processor, until they become a crumbly mixture. Roll the dough into a rectangle of 30 x 80cm (12 x 32ins), on a lightly floured surface. Divide the dough into two long rectangular halves of 30 x 40cm (12 x 16ins). On each half, sprinkle on half of the cinnamon–sugar mixture and half of the chopped pecans. Make sure the filling is evenly distributed over the entire dough. Using a rolling pin, lightly roll over the dough to press in the filling. Roll up each rectangle into a tight 40cm–long (16ins) log. Wrap each log in plastic and freeze for about 45 minutes until reasonably firm, so that it is easy to cut. Cut each the log into 10–12 pieces, depending on how thick you like your scrolls. In the meantime, smear the butter on the bottom of two 22cm–long (11ins) heavy pans (7-9cm (2.5 x 3.6ins) deep and preferably non-stick) and sprinkle the raw sugar and arrange the whole pecans face-side down. Lay the slices spiral side down, snugly touching each other.

SECOND/FINAL RISE (4–6 HOURS AT ROOM TEMPERATURE): Rise the scrolls until almost doubled, at a comfortable room temperature, around 20–25°C (68–77°F). Make sure the dough is covered, or mist frequently with water, to prevent drying.

PREHEAT YOUR OVEN TO 200°C (400°F)

BAKE: Bake for about 10 minutes, then reduce the oven to 180°C (350°F) for a further 15–20 minutes. If you are unsure whether the scrolls have cooked through, turn the oven off, and let them sit in the oven for a further 10 minutes. Remove pans from oven, and immediately invert the scrolls onto a large plate before the caramel hardens and the sticky scrolls will be stuck in the pans. Be careful of the dripping hot caramel, taking care not to burn yourself!

SOURDOUGH HOT CROSS BUNS

The idea for this recipe came about via a few requests I received from my students. Hot cross buns are such a big part of Easter celebration. With this recipe, I have created an especially delicious sourdough hot cross buns that are soft, rich in spices and studded with sultanas and currants. If you like, you can add 75g (2 ½oz) of finely chopped glacé orange peel. Yum! You will be very popular at Eastertime.

INGREDIENTS

200g (7oz) active white wheat or spelt sourdough starter
400g (14oz) full cream organic yoghurt (straight from the fridge or at room temperature in winter time)
225–250g (8–9oz) filtered water
900g (32oz) white spelt or wheat flour

100g (3½oz) raw organic sugar
50g (1¾oz) organic butter
2 teaspoons organic cinnamon powder
2–3 teaspoons mixed spice
3 teaspoons sea-salt
250g (9oz) sultanas
150g (5oz) currants

METHOD

Soak sultanas and currants in ¼ cup of filtered water for a couple hours, drain before using.

MEASURE INGREDIENTS (2–3 MINS): Use, preferably, a digital scale, to weigh all ingredients. Then put all ingredients, except soaked sultanas in a non-metallic bowl, starting with starter and yoghurt then the rest of the ingredients and lastly the salt.

MIX INGREDIENTS (2–3 MINS): Using a spatula or a wooden spoon, stir the ingredients together until they form a cohesive mass.

REST (15–20 MINS)

KNEADING – AIR KNEADING (10–15 MINS): Using your fingertips, throw your dough into the air and then slap/throw it onto your bench. After you have done this for about 10 minutes, the dough will develop some elasticity. This is a soft, rather than elastic, dough. You may find it easier to lightly spray oil on your bench and your hands. The more kneading, the finer the crumb of this bread will be.

REST (20–30 MINS): Your dough should feel soft and slightly sticky, but it will not be as elastic as a bread dough.

DO THE WINDOWPANE TEST: See 'Sourdough Bread Making Step-by-Step'.

FIRST RISE (2 HOURS): Gather your dough together and shape into a ball. Let it rest in a non-metallic container or a bowl, covered with a wet tea-towel or wet cling wrap. Let your dough rise to about one and a quarter times its size—the time taken will vary.

ADD (5 MINS): Add the soaked sultanas and knead to distribute.

DIVIDE AND SHAPE (5 MINS): Divide and shape the dough into 100–125g (3 ½–4oz) pieces, then round off each dough piece into a tight ball. Brush with milk, single cream or egg wash, if desired. Place the buns, snuggled close together, in a buttered, non-stick, deep lamington (24 x 34cm (9.6 x 13.6in) and 5–6cm (2–2 ½oz)) pan.

SECOND/FINAL RISE (ABOUT 4–8 HOURS): Rise until almost doubled, at a comfortable room temperature, around 20–25°C (68–77°F) Make sure the dough is covered, or mist with water, to prevent drying.

PREHEAT YOUR OVEN TO 205°C (400°F).

BAKE: Bake for about 5 minutes, then reduce the oven to 185°C (365°F) for a further 15–20 minutes until browned and cooked through. If you are unsure whether the buns have cooked through, turn the oven off, and let the loaves sit in the oven for a further 10 minutes. Remove the pan from oven and invert the buns onto a cooling rack. Once the buns are cooled, pipe a white sugar icing onto the buns to form a cross.

WITHOUT THE ICING, BUNS ARE SUITABLE FOR FREEZING AND WILL KEEP FOR A COUPLE OF MONTHS FROZEN.

Sourdough Hot Cross Buns

Coffee & Walnut Loaf

COFFEE & WALNUT LOAF

MAKES 2 MEDIUM-TINNED LOAVES OR 3 FREE-FORMED LOAVES

Who could resist the smell of this coffee and walnut loaf as it is baking? This recipe makes two impressive loaves. I love to eat a toasted slice of this loaf spread with a cream cheese, such as mascarpone. It is just so delicious without being overly sweet at all, need I say more?

INGREDIENTS

200g (7oz) active whole wheat or spelt starter
   sourdough starter
425g (15oz) full cream organic milk
100g (3½oz) strong espresso
900g (32oz) white wheat or spelt flour, where
   the coarse bran has been sifted (you may
   need to do this yourself)
75g (2½oz) agave syrup, maple syrup or 100g

(3½oz) sugar
25g (¾oz) vanilla bean paste
25g (¾oz) sea salt
200g (7oz) walnuts, coarsely chopped
   (organic, if possible)
250g (5oz) sultanas
30ml (1fl oz) of rum or water
Coffee sugar crystals for a crunchy topping.

METHOD

Soak sultanas in rum or water for 2 hours, then drain.

MEASURE INGREDIENTS (2–3 MINS): Use, preferably, a digital scale, to weigh all ingredients. Put all ingredients in a non-metallic bowl, except walnuts and sultanas, starting with starter and milk then the rest of the ingredients and lastly the salt.

MIX INGREDIENTS (2–3 MINS): Using a spatula or a wooden spoon, stir the ingredients together until they form a cohesive mass.

REST (15–20 MINS)

KNEADING – AIR KNEADING (5 MINS): Using your fingertips, throw your dough into the air and then slap/throw it onto your bench. After you have done this for about 5 minutes, the dough will have developed some elasticity. You may find it easier to lightly spray oil onto your bench and your hands.

REST (20–30 MINS): Your dough should feel soft and slightly sticky. This dough will not have the elasticity of bread dough.

DO THE WINDOWPANE TEST: See 'Sourdough Bread Making Step-by-Step'.

FIRST RISE (2 HOURS AT ROOM TEMPERATURE): Gather your dough together and shape into a ball. Let it rest in a non-metallic container or a bowl covered with a wet tea towel or wet cling wrap. Let your dough rise to about one and a quarter times its size—the time taken will vary.

ADD: Knead in chopped walnuts and sultanas and mix well to evenly distribute them.

DIVIDE AND SHAPE (5 MINS): Divide and shape the dough as desired. This recipe will fit into two medium tins. Brush the top of each loaf with water or milk, and if desired, generously sprinkle some sugar crystals on top of each loaf, which will caramelise and give the loaves a sweet crunchy crust.

SECOND/FINAL RISE: Rise again until almost doubled, at a comfortable room temperature around 20–25°C (68–77°F). Make sure the dough is covered or mist with water to prevent drying. Do the indentation test–see 'Sourdough Bread Making Step-by-Step'.

PREHEAT YOUR OVEN TO 225ºC (437ºF)

BAKE: Bake for about 5 minutes, then reduce the oven to 185°C (365°F) for a further 25–30 minutes until browned and cooked. These loaves will look quite dark because of the dark brown colouring from the coffee. If you are unsure whether the loaves have cooked through, turn the oven off, and let the loaves sit in the oven for a further 10 minutes. Remove loaves from oven, taking care not to burn yourself!

REST: Let loaf cool before cutting.

SUITABLE FOR FREEZING AND WILL KEEP FOR A COUPLE OF MONTHS FROZEN.

SOURDOUGH 'EUROPEAN' DOUGHNUT

MAKES 10-12 DOUGHNUTS

My early memories of doughnuts were of chocolate ganache-filled Dutch donuts made by my Dutch-speaking grand auntie. This recipe is an adaptation of her yeasted doughnut recipe. This versatile sourdough doughnut can be shaped into the ring-shaped doughnuts rolled in cinnamon sugar or rounded into 'ball' donuts, which once cooked can be filled with chocolate ganache, custard or home-made jam.

INGREDIENTS

200g (7oz) thin and active white starter culture (1:1 flour to water ratio)
200g (7oz) filtered water, at room temperature
500g (17½oz) organic unbleached white wheat flour (strong gluten of 11–12 per cent)
50g (1¾oz) caster or icing sugar
1 egg
50g (1¾oz) butter
2 teaspoons sea-salt, finely ground

CHOCOLATE GANACHE: Melt equal amounts of organic butter and organic dark couverture chocolate (55–70 per cent cocoa), mix well. Add organic icing sugar to the chocolate butter mixture, until you achieve the desired consistency, a thick paste.

CHOCOLATE ICING: As per ganache, but add less icing sugar so the mixture is like a crepe batter. Ice the doughnuts while still hot to achieve the shiny glazed look.

METHOD

MEASURE INGREDIENTS (2–3 MINS): Use, preferably, a digital scale, to weigh all ingredients. Put all ingredients, except butter, in a non-metallic bowl.

MIX INGREDIENTS (2–3 MINS): Using a spatula or a wooden spoon, stir the ingredients together until they form a cohesive mass.

REST (20 MINS)

ADD BUTTER AND KNEAD (20–25 MINS): Using a spatula or a wooden spoon, knead in the butter into the rest of the dough. This dough is not a wet dough, it will have a non-sticky feel, but will be soft. You can do normal dough kneading rather than the air kneading method. Either method is fine. After 10–15 minutes of kneading, the dough will be elastic and soft. The more kneading this dough receives, the finer the texture of your donuts.

REST (20–30 MINS)

FIRST RISE (2–3 HOURS): Scoop all the dough back into the oiled bowl. Allow the dough to rise, covered with wet cling wrap or a tea towel. The dough will rise by about 50 per cent, but do not over-rise.

DIVIDE AND SHAPE: Dust your bench generously with flour. Invert the dough onto the bench. Divide the dough into 12–14 pieces (approx. 80–90g/2 ½–3oz each), round each piece gently with your hand to form tight small balls. Rest the dough balls for about 15 minutes to relax the gluten. If you want a ring doughnut, poke your index finger into the centre of the ball of dough and swing the dough around your index finger until you have a reasonable size hole in the middle and the ball looks like a large ring of dough (as for bagel). Don't worry about making too big a hole in the middle, the dough will come in together as it is rising, closing the hole slightly. Spray two baking trays with olive oil and spray each doughnut generously with oil to stop it drying out, and place each doughnut 2cm (¾in) apart onto the baking tray.

FINAL RISE ABOUT (2–4 HOURS): Let the doughnuts rise again until they increase their size by 50 per cent again. The donuts will look flat at this stage. Do not over-rise and do not reshape the doughnut, the flat shaped doughnuts will puff up to become a round ball in the hot oil.

FRY: About 30 minutes before the doughnut is ready, fill a deep saucepan (20–24cm/8–10ins diameter) with grapeseed oil, olive oil or ghee. Heat the oil until it reaches a medium–high heat, then reduce the heat. Using a large, round slotted spoon, gently drop 2–3 doughnuts into the hot oil. Using the slotted spoon to flip them, fry the doughnuts until cooked and brown. Do not flip doughnut in the first 3–5 minutes or it will not puff up to a round ball. You may reduce the temperature to 165°C (329°F) while the doughnuts are cooking. Cook until they are a caramel colour, a shade darker than golden brown. This will take a while, be patient and watch the oil temperature conscientiously. Remove the doughnuts carefully with the slotted spoon, draining off all the oil before placing them onto absorbent paper. After about a minute, roll the doughnuts into a mixture of 150g (5oz) caster sugar and 50g (5oz) icing sugar and 1 teaspoon of cinnamon OR you can inject the doughnuts with chocolate ganache, custard or jam using a piping bag fitted with a round pipping nozzle. Enjoy!

NOT SUITABLE TO FREEZE, BEST EATEN WARM.

Sourdough 'European' Doughnuts

Pear and Almond Loaf

PEAR AND ALMOND LOAF

MAKES 2 MEDIUM-TINNED LOAVES OR 3 FREE-FORM LOAVES

The idea of combining pear and almond in a loaf came from my wonderful friend, Janet. She used to buy a pear and almond loaf for her children's after-school treat. But the bakery that used to make this loaf no longer exists. I think pear and almond works beautifully together, but the addition of vanilla or cardamom adds an extra dimension.

INGREDIENTS

200g (7oz) wholemeal wheat or spelt culture, ripe and at room temperature
800g (28oz) organic unbleached white wheat or spelt flour
480g (16oz) pear juice at room temperature
3 tablespoons concentrated pear juice
50g (1¾oz) raw organic sugar (optional)

3 teaspoons sea-salt, finely ground
½ tablespoon vanilla bean extract or 1 ½ teaspoons ground cardamon

FILLINGS

200g (7oz) lightly toasted whole almonds
200–250g (7–9oz) dried pear, quartered

METHOD

MEASURE INGREDIENTS (2–3 MINS): Use, preferably, a digital scale, to weigh all ingredients in a non-metallic bowl, except the fillings, starting with liquids, flour and lastly the salt.

MIX INGREDIENTS (2–3 MINS): Using a spatula or a wooden spoon, stir the ingredients together until they form a cohesive mass.

REST (15–20 MINS)

KNEADING – AIR KNEADING (10–15 MINS): Using your fingertips, throw your dough into the air and then slap/throw it onto your bench. After you have done this for about 5 minutes, the dough will have developed some elasticity. This is a soft, rather than elastic, dough, but you will develop elasticity if you continue to knead for an extra 10 minutes.

REST (20–30 MINS): This dough will develop some elasticity, but is mostly a soft, slightly sticky dough.

DO THE WINDOW PANE TEST: See 'Sourdough Bread Making Step-by-Step'.

FIRST RISE (ABOUT 1 HOUR IN WARM WEATHER AND 2 HOURS IN COLD WEATHER): Leave the dough to rise in a covered container, at a comfortable room temperature, around 20–25°C (68–77°F).

DOUGH RETARDATION (OPTIONAL, OVERNIGHT): Cover the dough and leave the dough in the fridge overnight. The next day, take the dough out of the fridge and leave to thaw for about an hour.

TURNING/FOLDING: See 'Sourdough Bread Making Step-by-Step'. After turning/folding, let the dough sit for 10–15 minutes to relax the gluten.

DIVIDE AND SHAPE (5 MINS): Divide the dough into two pieces. Flatten each piece into a rough rectangle shape, place and distribute evenly half of the almonds and pear on top of the dough. Roll tightly and tuck in at the sides. This recipe will fit into two medium tins (10 x 23.5cm (4 x 9.4in) and 10cm (4in) deep) or make two free-form loaves. Mist the loaves with water and sprinkle with some chopped almonds if desired.

SECOND/FINAL RISE (4–6 HOURS AT ROOM TEMPERATURE): Rise the shaped loaves until almost doubled, at a comfortable room temperature around 20–25°C (68–77°F) Make sure the dough is covered or mist with water frequently to prevent drying.

PREHEAT YOUR OVEN TO 225°C (437°F)

BAKE: Bake for about 10 minutes, then reduce the oven to 215°C (419°F) for a further 25–35 minutes. If you are unsure whether the loaves have cooked through, turn the oven off, and let the loaves sit in the oven for a further 10 minutes. Remove loaves from oven, taking care not to burn yourself!

REST: Let the bread cool before cutting.

SUITABLE FOR FREEZING AND WILL KEEP FOR A COUPLE OF MONTHS FROZEN.

BATTER BREADS:

FROM CRUMPETS TO CRÊPES

PERFECT SOURDOUGH CRUMPETS

MAKES 8 10CM-ROUND CRUMPETS

Tania, my student, dear friend, and Perth Royal Show serial winner, inspired me to create this recipe, because of her passion for wanting to make crumpets, her favourite breakfast bread. She no longer buys crumpets because commercial crumpets contain additives. This is my sourdough version and it is almost as light as the commercial version. I find I prefer to toast yesterday's crumpets. Toasting seems to bring out the caramelized flavour of the crispy crust. I found the most perfect crumpet ring at my local kitchenware shop, it is a stainless steel egg ring of 10cm (4 inches) diameter and 2.5cm (1 inch) high with a handle (see Equipment). Don't try making these with silicone egg rings as they prevent the crumpets from cooking evenly as the sides will not cook. NOTE: For wholemeal crumpets, replace white flour with wholemeal flour and add an extra 50-100g (1 ¾-3 ½oz) water to this recipe.

INGREDIENTS

STEP 1: 6-12 HOURS PRIOR TO MAKING THE CRUMPET BATTER
50g (1¾oz) active rye starter
300g (10½oz) organic white flour (spelt or wheat)

450–500g (15½ –17oz) filtered water (lukewarm water if the weather is cold)

Mix well and leave covered in a warm place. This starter mixture should have the consistency of a thick pancake batter. It is ready when the starter mixture is bubbly. If the mixture is too thick then stir in a small amount of additional water to attain the correct consistency.

STEP 2: MAKING THE CRUMPET BATTER
600g (21oz) active starter from step 1
1 teaspoon sea-salt

2 teaspoons raw organic sugar (optional)
1 teaspoon bicarbonate soda

METHOD

MIX INGREDIENTS (2–3 MINS): Using a hand/electric whisk, briefly whisk all ingredients together. The mixture will be frothy and look like thick cream.

COOK THE CRUMPETS: Heat up a (preferably non-stick) cast-iron griddle or sauté pan. If using a normal cast-iron pan, make sure you butter or oil your pan generously to prevent sticking just before you add the batter to the pan. I find that if I butter the pan while it is heating up, the butter tends to burn. Prepare each crumpet ring by smearing its side generously with butter. Place the crumpet rings on the pan. Wait till the pan and the rings are hot but not smoky, about 5–10 minutes. Pour the crumpet batter into the ring, about two-thirds full. Reduce the heat to medium–low. Let cook for about 8–10 minutes, during which time small bubbles will appear all over the surface of the crumpet. The crumpet is ready to be flipped when the top surface of the crumpet looks translucent or cooked, leaving a 1–2cm (½–¾in) area of raw batter in the middle of the crumpet. The side will shrink a little and pull away from the ring. Take the ring off each crumpet. Once flipped, cook the crumpet for a further 2–3 minutes until golden on the surface. Traditionally, crumpets are eaten toasted to give them extra crunchiness.

SUITABLE FOR FREEZING AND WILL KEEP FOR A COUPLE OF MONTHS FROZEN.

Perfect Sourdough Crumpets.

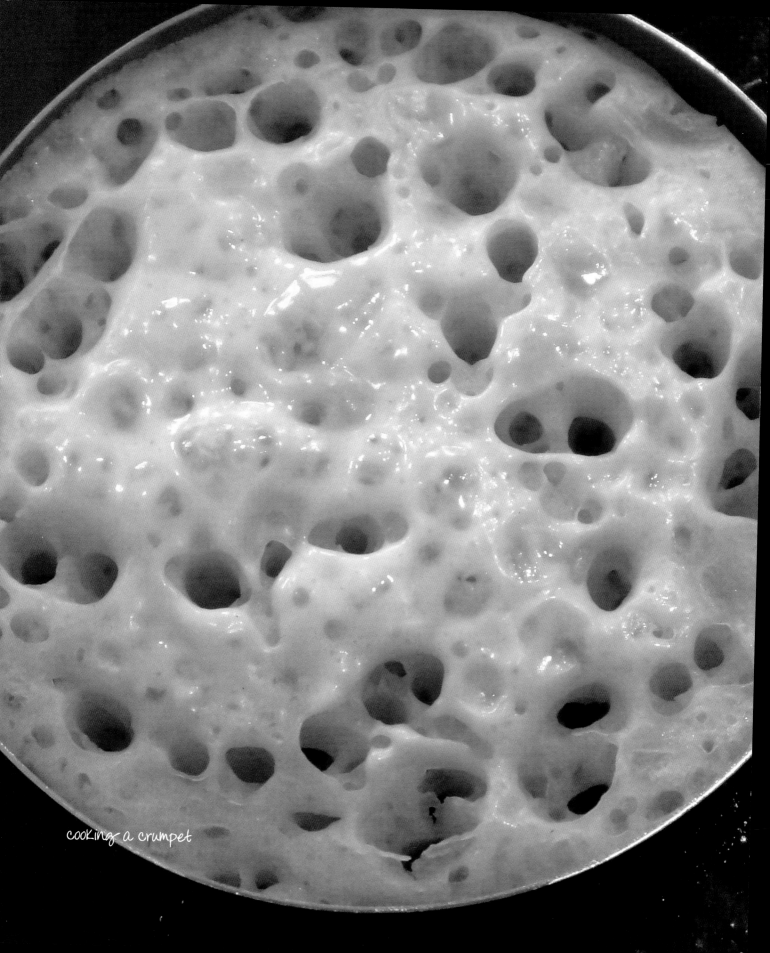

cooking a crumpet

SOURDOUGH WAFFLES

MAKES 8 18CM-ROUND WAFFLES

I have always loved the delicious taste and seductive aroma of waffles topped with vanilla bean ice-cream, walnuts and maple syrup, so much so that I bought an electric waffle maker last year. This is my take on waffles using sourdough, it will give you a more-ish crisp waffle and you won't believe how easy they are to make.

STEP 1: START 6-12 HOURS PRIOR TO MAKING THE WAFFLE BATTER

25g (¾oz) active rye starter

100g (3½oz) organic white wheat or spelt flour

200g (7oz) filtered water (lukewarm water if the weather is cold)

Mix well, and leave covered in a warm place. This starter mixture should have a consistency of a thick pancake batter. It is ready when the starter mixture is bubbly. If the mixture is too thick then stir in a small amount of additional water to attain the correct consistency.

STEP 2: MAKING THE WAFFLE BATTER

300g (10½oz) bubbly active starter, from step 1 (there will be a little left over)

120g (4oz) eggs, weighed without shells (about 3 large eggs)

50g (1¾oz) full cream and thick sour cream

80g (2½oz) flour

1 teaspoon salt

2 tablespoons raw organic sugar or honey

1 teaspoon vanilla bean paste or extract

50g (1¾oz) melted butter for cooking the waffles

Additional milk if mixture is too thick

METHOD

MEASURE INGREDIENTS (2–3 MINS): Use, preferably, a digital scale, to weigh all ingredients. Put all ingredients in a non-metallic bowl, starting with eggs, starter, and cream, then the rest of the ingredients and lastly the salt.

MIX INGREDIENTS (3 MINS): Using a hand/electric whisk, whisk all ingredients together for three minutes until well mixed. The mixture will look like pourable cream.

FIRST AND FINAL RISE UNTIL DOUBLED (ABOUT 3–4 HOURS): Make sure the batter is well-covered. Rise the waffle batter at a comfortable room temperature, around 20–25°C (68–77°F). The batter will double and become very frothy.

COOK THE WAFFLES: Heat up a cast-iron waffle iron. Make sure you butter or oil your pan generously to prevent sticking just before you add the batter. If using an electric waffle maker, follow the manufacturer's instructions. Wait till the waffle iron is hot, but not smoky. Pouring waffle batter into a hot waffle iron will stop the waffles from sticking. Pour the waffle batter to about half of the height of the waffle iron. Do not over-fill as the batter will over-flow and make a very difficult sticky mess to clean. Reduce heat to half (medium—low). Let cook for about 3-5 minutes, until cooked and golden brown. After a couple of waffles, you will work out how much batter to use and how long to cook the waffle. Repeat the process until all batter is used. Eat immediately while still warm.

ENGLISH MUFFINS

MAKES ABOUT 16 9CM-ROUND MUFFINS

Almost every man, woman and child loves the deliciousness and comfort that savouring an English muffins brings. It is a very unnerving experience to go and buy commercial English muffins because they are so full of additives, preservatives and things that should not belong inside our tummies! So, here is my sourdough English muffin recipe. They are satisfyingly delicious with a soft crumb and crusty crust when toasted and a buttery tanginess. These 'traditional' English muffins will satisfy everyone, plus you don't even need an oven to cook them. English muffins are traditionally eaten like crumpets. You can also make wholemeal ones if you like.

INGREDIENTS

150g (5oz) active white wheat or spelt
    sourdough starter
400g (14oz) full cream organic yoghurt
    (straight from the fridge or at room
    temperature in winter time)
200–225g (7–8oz) filtered water*

900g (32oz) white spelt or wheat flour
1 tablespoon sea-salt
Brown rice flour or fine polenta for dusting
    the muffins
*you will need 225g–250g (8–9oz) water if you
    are using all wholemeal flour

METHOD

MEASURE INGREDIENTS (2–3 MINS): Use, preferably, a digital scale, to weigh all ingredients. Put all ingredients in a non-metallic bowl, starting with water, starter and yoghurt, then the rest of the ingredients and lastly the salt.

MIX INGREDIENTS (2–3 MINS): Using a spatula or a wooden spoon, stir the ingredients together until they form a cohesive mass.

REST (20 MINS):

KNEADING – AIR KNEADING (15–20 MINS): Using your fingertips, throw your dough into the air and then slap/throw it onto your bench. After you have done this for about 5 minutes, the dough will develop some elasticity. This is a soft, rather than elastic, dough, but you will develop elasticity if you continue to knead for an extra 10–15 minutes. You may find it easier to oil your bench and your hands.

REST (20-30 MINS): Your dough should feel soft, elastic and slightly sticky.

ADJUST FLOUR OR WATER IF NECESSARY: If after the 30 minutes rest period your dough still feels too wet or too dry, then this is the time to add more water or flour.

FINAL KNEADING (5 MINS ONLY IF YOU ARE ADJUSTING FLOUR/WATER)

DO THE WINDOW PANE TEST: See 'Sourdough Bread Making Step-by-Step'.

FIRST RISE (1-2 HOURS OPTIONAL IN WARMER WEATHER): Gather your dough together and shape into a ball. Let it rest in a non-metallic container or a bowl covered with a wet tea towel or wet cling wrap. Let your dough rise to about one and a quarter times its size—the time taken will vary. You can also put this dough straight into the fridge without this first rise when the ambient temperature is warm (28°C/82°F and above).

DOUGH RETARDATION (OVERNIGHT): Leave dough in a covered container and leave the dough in the fridge, overnight. The next day, take the dough out of the fridge and leave to thaw for about an hour.

DIVIDE AND SHAPE: Heavily flour your bench and then cut the dough in half. Cover half of the dough and place the rest of the dough onto the floured surface. Dust a French (long, 45cm (18in)) rolling pin and roll out the dough until it is approximately 2cm (0.8in) thick. Allow the rolled out dough to rest slightly, so it does not spring back or shrink when you cut the muffins. Use a 9cm (3.6in) biscuit cutter to cut rounds from the dough. Slide a dough scraper under the dough rounds and place on a tray that has been heavily dusted with brown rice flour or fine polenta. Repeat with the remaining dough until you have used up all the dough. Dust the top of the muffins with brown rice flour. Reshape any leftover dough into a ball, roll out and cut out additional muffins.

RISE: Cover the muffins with baking paper and a wet tea towel or an over-sized plastic container. Allow to rise for 1–2 hours until slightly risen (about one and a quarter–one and a half times its original size—do not over-rise). The muffins will rise some more during cooking.

COOK: Heat a large frypan or sauté pan over a moderate heat. Carefully slide the muffins into the pan, ensuring they retain their shape. Cook for 10 minutes, checking towards the end of this time to ensure that the bottom of the muffin is not burning. The muffins will rise slightly and start to dome on the top. Flip the muffins over and apply gentle pressure with a spatula to flatten the muffin against the pan. Allow to cook for a further 5–8 minutes. Remove the muffin from the pan and allow to cool on a wire rack. Split in half and enjoy with lashings of butter (toasted or not!).

SUITABLE FOR FREEZING AND WILL KEEP FOR A COUPLE OF MONTHS FROZEN.

English Muffins

English Muffins

SOURDOUGH CRÊPES

MAKES 8 20CM-ROUND CRÊPES

My daughter loves crepes with chocolate ganache, so much so that I used to make these crepes for her every day for breakfast! The batter of this crepe is much thinner than what you probably have made before but this is what makes them lacy and light.

STEP 1: START 6-12 HOURS PRIOR TO MAKING THE CRÊPE BATTER

25g (¾oz) active rye starter

60g (2oz) organic white wheat or spelt flour

250g (8½oz) milk (lukewarm water if the weather is cold)

Mix well, and leave covered in a warm place. This starter mixture should have a consistency of a thin pancake batter. It is ready when the starter mixture is bubbly.

STEP 2

300g (10½oz) bubbly active starter, from steo 1 (there will be some left over)

25g (¾oz) potato flour

150g (5oz) eggs, weighed without shells (about 4 large eggs)

1 teaspoon salt

½ teaspoon bicarbonate soda (optional)

25g (¾oz) melted butter

Additional 50g (1¾oz) melted butter for cooking the crêpes

Additional milk, if mixture is too thick

METHOD

MEASURE INGREDIENTS (2–3 MINS): Use, preferably, a digital scale, to weigh all ingredients, then put all ingredients in a non-metallic bowl.

MIX INGREDIENTS (3 MINS): Using a hand/electric whisk, whisk all ingredients together for three minutes until well mixed the mixture should be the consistency of thin cream, if not, whisk in more milk.

COOK THE CRÊPES: Heat up a crêpe pan or a shallow sauté pan if you do not have a crêpe pan. Add 2–3 teaspoons of melted butter to the crêpe pan and melt until very hot but not smoky. Pour 2–3 tablespoons of batter into the pan, turning and rotating the pan so the crêpe batter covers the whole surface of the pan. Cook until the crêpe is browned, about 2–3 minutes. Toss the crêpe or turn with a flat silicon or wooden spatula and brown the other side (about 1 minute). Transfer to a plate and keep warm. Repeat the process until all batter is used. Eat immediately while still warm.

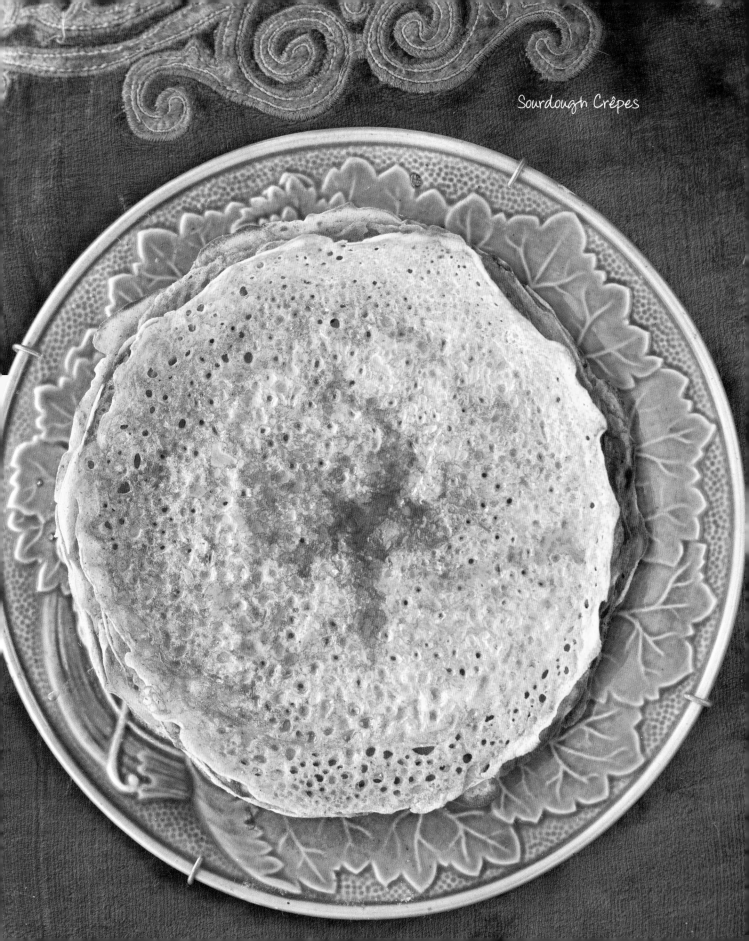

Sourdough Crêpes

Chinese Steam Sourdough Bun

STEAM BUNS

CHINESE STEAM SOURDOUGH BUNS

One of the earliest memories I have of my grandmother is being around her, making and eating food. My grandma makes the most divine Chinese steam buns. Steam buns can be plain or filled with sweet black sesame paste, peanut and palm sugar or savoury ones can be filled with barbecue pork or minced soya chicken. My favourite way of eating steam buns is to eat them with a filling of twice-cooked pork., a tradition my mother continues.

INGREDIENTS

150g (5oz) active white wheat or spelt
  sourdough starter
225g (8oz) water
400g (14oz) full cream organic yoghurt
  (straight from the fridge or at room
  temperature in winter time)

900g (32oz) white spelt or wheat flour
30g (1oz) agave syrup or 50g (1¾oz) raw
  sugar
50g (1¾oz) butter, softened
1 tablespoon sea-salt

METHOD

MEASURE INGREDIENTS (2–3 MINS): Use, preferably, a digital scale, to weigh all ingredients. Put all ingredients, except butter, in a non-metallic bowl, starting with starter and yoghurt then the rest of the ingredients and lastly the salt.

MIX INGREDIENTS (2–3 MINS): Using a spatula or a wooden spoon, stir the ingredients together until they form a cohesive mass.

REST (15–20 MINS)

KNEADING – AIR KNEADING (15 MINS): Using your fingertips, throw your dough into the air and then slap/throw it onto your bench. After you have done this for about 5 minutes, the dough will have developed some elasticity. This is a soft, rather than elastic, dough but you will develop elasticity if you continue to knead for an extra 10 minutes. You may find it easier to lightly oil your bench and your hands.

REST (20–30 MINS): This dough will develop some elasticity, but is mostly a soft, slightly sticky dough.

ADD (5 MINS): Add softened butter and gently knead the dough for another 5 minutes until butter is well incorporated.

DO THE WINDOWPANE TEST: See 'Sourdough Bread Making Step-by-Step'.

FIRST RISE (1–2 HOURS): Gather your dough together and shape into a ball. Let it rest in a non-metallic container or a bowl covered with a wet tea towel or wet cling wrap. Let your dough rise to about one and a quarter times its size—the time taken will vary. Do not cut this step out or the buns will not rise.

DOUGH RETARDATION (OPTIONAL, OVERNIGHT): Cover the dough and leave the dough in the fridge overnight. The next day, take the dough out of the fridge and leave to thaw for about an hour.

TURNING/FOLDING: See 'Sourdough Bread Making Step-by-Step'. After turning/folding, let the dough sit for 10–15 minutes to relax the gluten.

DIVIDE AND SHAPE (5 MINS): Divide and shape the dough into 100–120g (3 ½–4oz) pieces, no larger as your buns will not cook through, then round each dough piece into a tight ball. Place the individual buns onto a square piece of baking paper. Alternatively, you can snuggle a few of these buns together, like pull-apart loaf. Place the buns inside your choice of steamer.

SECOND/FINAL RISE ABOUT (2–4 HOURS): Allow the buns to rise until almost doubled at a comfortable room temperature, around 20–25°C (68–77°F). Make sure the dough is covered, or mist with water, to prevent drying. Do not over-rise dough or it will deflate during steaming. If you are not sure, rise the dough until it is just larger than one and a half times its original size.

STEAM: Steam the buns for about 20–30 minutes, depending on size. Remove buns from steamer, taking care not to burn yourself with the hot steam! If using an electric steam oven, set the oven to 100°C (212°F). Do not forget to preheat your steam oven for half an hour before steaming or follow the manufacturer's manual. (Bamboo or stainless steel steamers also work really well.)

SUITABLE FOR FREEZING AND WILL KEEP FOR A COUPLE OF MONTHS FROZEN. THAW OUT COMPLETELY AND RE-STEAM THE BUNS FOR 10–15 MINUTES TO REFRESH.

Chinese Steam Sourdough Buns

Maple Wholemeal Sourdough Buns

MAPLE WHOLEMEAL SOURDOUGH BUNS

MAKES ABOUT 12-16 BUNS

Maple syrup gives these wholemeal buns a really beautiful and distinctive sweet caramel aroma. Maple syrup is full of anti-oxidants and minerals. Replace maple syrup with honey or agave syrup if you like.

INGREDIENTS

150g (5oz) active white wheat or spelt
    sourdough
225g (8oz) water
400g (14oz) full cream organic yoghurt
    (straight from the fridge or at room
    temperature in winter time)

450g (15½oz) white spelt or wheat flour
450g (15½oz) wholemeal wheat or spelt flour
100g (3½oz) maple syrup
50g (1¾oz) butter, softened
1 tablespoon sea-salt

METHOD

MEASURE INGREDIENTS (2–3 MINS): Use, preferably, a digital scale, to weigh all ingredients. Put all ingredients, except butter, in a non-metallic bowl, starting with starter and yoghurt, then the rest of the ingredients and lastly the salt.

MIX INGREDIENTS (2–3 MINS): Using a spatula or a wooden spoon, stir the ingredients together until they form a cohesive mass.

REST (15–20 MINS)

KNEADING – AIR KNEADING (15 MINS): Using your fingertips, throw your dough into the air and then slap/throw it onto your bench. After you have done this for about 5 minutes, the dough will have developed some elasticity. This is a soft, rather than elastic, dough, but you will develop elasticity if you continue to knead for an extra 10 minutes. You may find it easier to lightly oil your bench and your hands.

REST (20–30 MINS): This dough will develop some elasticity, but is mostly a soft, slightly sticky dough.

ADD (5 MINS): Add softened butter and gently knead the dough for another 5 minutes until butter is incorporated.

DO THE WINDOWPANE TEST: See 'Sourdough Bread Making Step-by-Step'.

FIRST RISE (1–2 HOURS): Gather your dough together and shape into a ball, let it rest in a covered non-metallic container or a bowl covered with a wet tea towel or wet cling wrap. Let your dough rise to about one and a quarter times its size—the time taken will vary. Do not cut this step out or the buns will not rise.

DOUGH RETARDATION (OPTIONAL, OVERNIGHT): Cover the dough and leave the dough in the fridge overnight. The next day, take the dough out of the fridge and leave to thaw for about an hour.

TURNING/FOLDING: See 'Sourdough Bread Making Step-by-Step'. After turning/folding, let the dough sit for 10–15 minutes to relax the gluten.

DIVIDE AND SHAPE (5 MINS): Divide and shape the dough into 100–120g (3 ½–4oz) pieces, no larger as your buns will not cook through, then round each dough piece into a tight ball. Place the individual buns onto a square piece of baking paper. Alternatively, you can snuggle a few of these buns together, like pull-apart loaf. Place the buns inside your choice of steamer.

SECOND/FINAL RISE ABOUT (2–4 HOURS): Allow the buns to rise until almost doubled at a comfortable room temperature, around 20–25°C (68–77°F). Make sure the dough is covered or mist with water to prevent drying. Do not over-rise dough or it will deflate during steaming, if you are not sure, rise the dough until it is just larger than one and a half times its original size.

STEAM: Steam the buns for about 20–30 minutes, depending on size. Remove buns from steamer, taking care not to burn yourself with the hot steam! If using an electric steam oven the temperature to set your steam oven is 100°C (200°) and do not forget to preheat your steam oven for 30 minutes before steaming or follow its manufacturer's manual. (Bamboo or stainless steel steamers also work really well.)

SUITABLE FOR FREEZING AND WILL KEEP FOR A COUPLE OF MONTHS FROZEN. THAW OUT COMPLETELY AND RE-STEAM THE BUNS FOR 10–15 MINUTES TO REFRESH.

Sweet Coconut Sourdough Buns

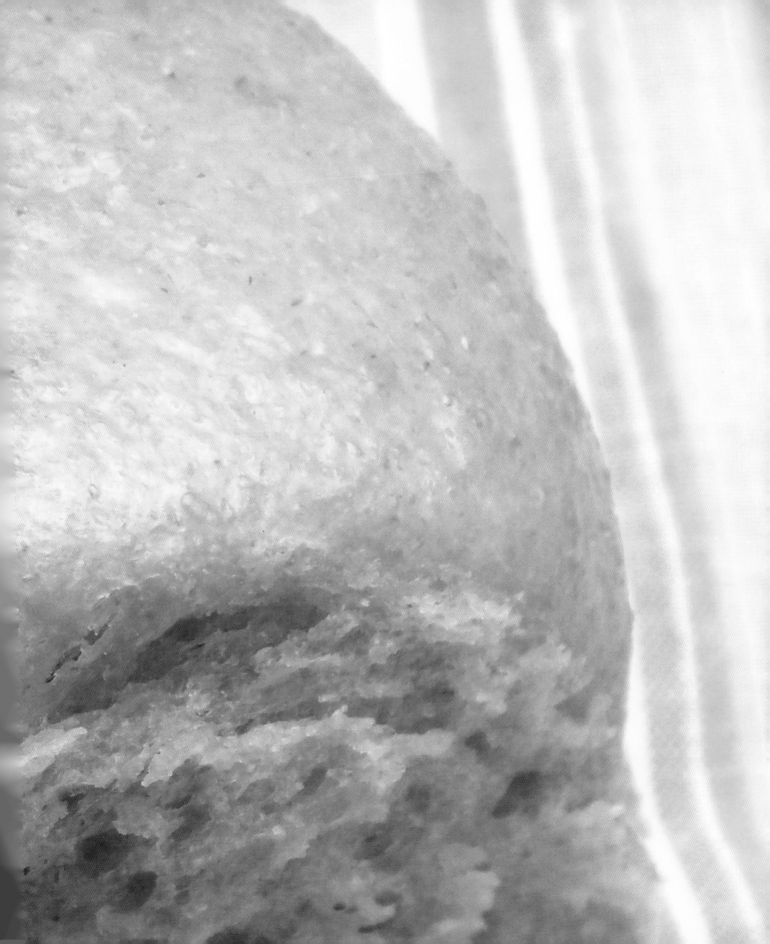

SWEET COCONUT SOURDOUGH BUNS

MAKES ABOUT 12-16 BUNS (VEGAN/DAIRY FREE)

The flavour of this mildly sweet coconut bun is just delightful. Opening a coconut requires a little bit of ingenuity and practice but you can find fresh coconut, tetra packed or canned coconut juice or frozen coconut juice at your local supermarket or asian grocers.

INGREDIENTS

150g (5oz) active white wheat or spelt
   sourdough starter
160–175g (5½–16oz) coconut water
400ml (13½fl oz) coconut milk
900g (32oz) white spelt or wheat flour

150–200g (7oz) palm sugar or jaggery or
   rapadura/panella sugar
50g (1¾oz) coconut oil, macadamia or
   grapeseed oil
1 tablespoon sea-salt

METHOD

MEASURE INGREDIENTS (2–3 MINS): Use, preferably, a digital scale, to weigh all ingredients. Put all ingredients, in a non-metallic bowl, starting with starter, then the rest of the ingredients and lastly, salt.

MIX INGREDIENTS (2–3 MINS): Using a spatula or a wooden spoon, stir the ingredients together until they form a cohesive mass.

REST (15–20 MINS)

KNEADING – AIR KNEADING (15 MINS): Using your fingertips, throw your dough into the air and then slap/throw it onto your bench. After you have done this for about 5 minutes, the dough will have developed some elasticity. This is a soft, rather than elastic, dough but you will develop elasticity if you continue to knead for an extra 10 minutes. You may find it easier to oil your bench and your hands.

REST (20–30 MINS): Your dough should feel soft, elastic and slightly sticky.

DO THE WINDOWPANE TEST: See 'Sourdough Bread Making Step-by-Step'.

FIRST RISE (1–2 HOURS): Gather your dough together and shape into a ball. Let it rest in a covered non-metallic container or a bowl covered with a wet tea towel or a wet cling wrap. Let your dough rise to about one and a quarter times its size—the time taken will vary. Do not cut this step out or the buns will not rise.

DOUGH RETARDATION (OPTIONAL, OVERNIGHT): Cover the dough and leave the dough in the fridge, overnight. The next day, take the dough out of the fridge and leave to thaw for about an hour.

TURNING/FOLDING: See 'Sourdough Bread Making Step-by-Step'. After turning/folding, let the dough sit for 10–15 minutes to relax the gluten.

DIVIDE AND SHAPE (5 MINS): Divide and shape the dough into 100–120g (3 ½–4oz) pieces (no larger as your buns will not cook through) then round each dough piece into a tight ball. Place the individual buns onto a square piece of baking paper. Alternatively, you can snuggle a few of these buns together, like pull-apart loaf. Place the buns inside your choice of steamer.

SECOND/FINAL RISE ABOUT (2–4 HOURS): Allow the buns to rise until almost doubled at a comfortable room temperature, around 20–25°C (68–77°). Make sure the dough is covered or mist with water to prevent drying. Do not over-rise dough or it will deflate during steaming. If you are not sure, rise the dough until it is just larger than one and a half times its original size.

STEAM: Steam the buns for about 20–30 mins, depending on size. Remove buns from steamer, taking care not to burn yourself with the hot steam! If using an electric steam oven, set your oven to 100°C (200°F). Do not forget to preheat your steam oven for half an hour before steaming or follow its manufacturer's manual. (Bamboo or stainless steel steamers also work really well.)

SUITABLE FOR FREEZING AND WILL KEEP FOR A COUPLE OF MONTHS FROZEN. THAW OUT COMPLETELY AND RE-STEAM THE BUNS FOR 10–15 MINUTES TO REFRESH.

SOURDOUGH CROISSANTS AND PASTRIES

INTRODUCTION

Although most people identify croissants with France, croissants were first baked by Viennese bakers in 1683, while Austria was being attacked by the Turks. When the Turks arrived in Vienna, they were tired and dug themselves a series of underground tunnels. The Viennese bakers who were up all night working in their underground bakeries heard the attackers, who were then caught by surprise and driven out from the city.

As a reward, Viennese bakers were given special privileges including the right to sell certain pastries at high prices. The bakers soon developed croissants, which mocked the crescent moon on the Turkish flag.

It wasn't until a hundred years later that the croissant was introduced into France by Marie-Antoinette. The croissants we love today did not become popular until the 1920s.

If you are using commercial yeast to leaven your 'white' croissant dough, you will get very light and airy, textured croissants. However, the best tasting croissants are sourdough croissants (albeit a little bit heavier compared to the yeasted ones). The lactobacteria in sourdough fermentation helps pre-digest butter in croissants.

Technical aspects of making croissants

Croissant dough is essentially a yeasted (or wild-yeasted, in the case of sourdough) flaky pastry. It is the link between a brioche dough and a flaky pastry dough—it is a brioche dough which has been given the flaky pastry treatment.

Making croissants is more akin to making pastry than making bread. This is an important point to note, because we do not want to 'knead' the dough, instead we do as little kneading as possible. The buttery flaky layers, characteristic of the croissant, are made by creating a series of layers of fat (butter) and dough. These layers are created by giving the dough a series of 'turns'. Each layer of dough is separated by butter. During baking, the layers of butter and dough will separate and puff up due to the giving off steam.

The classic technique of croissants requires four 'turns' in total, but three 'turns' is acceptable.

You won't believe how easy they are to make!

Important things to remember

The texture of the dough and the butter must be about equal—in other words, you cannot work hard butter on soft dough! Or vice versa.

Make sure that the butter does not melt into the dough—the butter needs to be soft but still chilled. It must still be slightly firm to the touch.

If your butter starts to soften and ooze/smear out of the dough as you are rolling it, quickly chill the dough in the fridge. The most important thing to remember is that the butter and dough need to move as one, in other words, their consistency has to be the same. Do not work (roll) the chilled dough if it is very cold and stiff, you will break the dough and create cracks that will let the butter ooze out. Any smears or cracks of butter seeping from the dough can be remedied with a generous sprinkle of flour.

Storing croissants

Croissants are best eaten straight from the oven. Fortunately, their low water/high fat content means that both raw croissants and baked croissants all freeze well.

Frozen, baked croissants should be put into a preheated 220°C (420°F) oven for 7–10 minutes and then moved to cool on a rack for 5 minutes before eating.

Frozen, raw croissants can be thawed overnight at room temperature, then once they have doubled in size, bake as per normal.

Croissant dough cross-section

Croissants

SOURDOUGH CROISSANT

MAKES 10 LARGE OR 14 SMALL CROISSANTS

My preference is to use a mixture of 50:50 unbleached white and wholemeal wheat or spelt flour. However, this recipe will also work well with either 100 per cent wholemeal or unbleached premium bakers flour (wheat/spelt). So, the choice is entirely yours! It is good to experiment with different types and proportions of flours to find the one you prefer. Wholemeal flour does not just add extra nutrients and fibre, it also gives the croissants a flakier texture with a hint of sweetness from the wholegrain. The crumb of wholemeal croissant will be heavier than a white croissant because it will not rise as much. White bakers flour gives the croissants a higher rise, due to its high gluten content. NOTE: The high amount of sugar in this recipe is necessary to reduce the acidity of the starter. However, this recipe will work just as well if you omit the sugar completely. Sugar-less croissants will have a noticeable tinge of acidity.

INGREDIENTS

225g (8oz) active wheat or spelt sourdough, white or wholemeal starter
500g (17½oz) organic wheat or spelt flour of your choice (see comments above) or:
50g (1¾oz) wholemeal spelt
250g (9oz) white spelt
200g (7oz) white wheat
150g (5oz) chilled water or milk or soy milk
(can be room temperature water in winter time)
100g (3oz) milk
organic egg
40–75g (1½–2 ½oz) organic caster sugar (see my comment above)
1½ teaspoons sea-salt
250g (9oz) organic butter

METHOD

MEASURE INGREDIENTS (2–3 MINS): Use, preferably, a digital scale, to weigh all ingredients including water. Put all ingredients in a non-metallic bowl, starting with the liquids then the rest of the ingredients, except butter, and lastly the salt.

MIX INGREDIENTS (2–3 MINS): Using a spatula or wooden spoon, stir the ingredients together until they form a cohesive mass.

REST (15–20 MINS)

KNEAD (3–4 MINS): Knead until the dough is just mixed, to one homogeneous colour. Do not over-work the dough, or your croissants will be tough and impossible to roll.

FIRST RISE (1–2 HOURS): Rise the dough in a covered container. The dough should rise a little.

DOUGH RETARDATION (OPTIONAL, OVERNIGHT): Cover the dough and leave the dough in the fridge, overnight.

NEXT DAY

PREPARE THE DOUGH: Take the dough out of the fridge, and thaw until the dough feels soft and pliable, but still cold to touch, about 1–2 hours depending on the ambient temperature.

PREPARE THE BUTTER: Take the butter out of the fridge for 10–15 minutes until it is malleable but still cold. Place the butter on a floured surface and sprinkle some flour on top. Using a rolling pin, flatten the butter to about 1cm (½in) thickness and make a rough square of 12 x 12cm (6ins).

CROISSANT DOUGH PREPARATION BEFORE THE 'TURNS': On a well-floured surface, roll the chilled dough with a rolling pin (a long one without handles, preferably), into a square of about 0.75cm (1/3in) thickness. Turn the square of dough slightly on an angle so that it is in the shape of a kite in front of you. Place the squared butter in the middle of the dough. Roll out the four triangle 'ears' surrounding the butter to about 0.5cm thickness. Fold each one of the thin 'ears', clockwise, over the top of the butter. Chill the dough/butter envelope for 10 minutes in a plastic container in the fridge or in the freezer for 5 minutes. Take the dough/butter envelope out of the fridge and while the dough is chilled but not hard, use the French rolling pin to roll the dough into a rectangle measuring around 20–25cm (8–10in) wide and 60–75cm (24–30in) long. Do not get too stressed in getting the right measurements, just do your best the first time. Believe me, after making this croissant dough two or three times, you will find this quite easy! Fold one third of the dough, farthest from you, to next third, and fold again like folding a business letter.

DOING THE TURNS

FIRST TURN: On a floured surface, put the spine of the dough 'book' on your left-hand side.

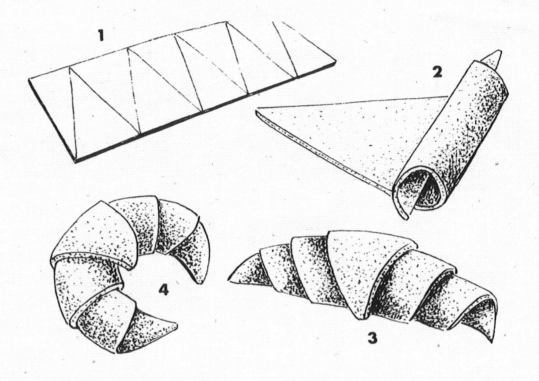

Roll the dough to about 75cm (30in) long (the width will follow the length, about 25–30cm (10–12in)). Always roll away from you. Fold one third of the dough, farthest from you, to the next third, and fold again like folding a business letter. Chill for 10-15 minutes in the fridge. Repeat this 'turn' 2–3 more times, chill in the fridge between turns. Your croissant dough is now ready.

SHAPE YOUR CROISSANTS: Roll the dough into a rectangle of 60 x 30cm (24 x 12in) and about 5mm thick. Cut into two pieces length ways; Cut each half into 7 triangles with a base of 15cm (6ins) (17.5 x 17.5 x 15cm (7 x 7 x 6ins) size (see diagram 1). You should have a total of 7 small croissants from each half, making up 14 croissants in total. Lay the croissants on a large baking tray and allow some room in between for expansion. Brush with an egg or milk glaze, if you like. Cover with a baking paper, then a wet towel or a heavy plastic tablecloth. Mist with water frequently to prevent sticking. During turning, take care not to smear the butter (dough is too warm) or crack the dough (dough is too cold/hard). If you do, just cover the exposed butter with a generous sprinkling of flour. See 'Sourdough Croissant' Introduction.

RISE: Leave the croissants to rise for a few hours at room temperature, until they double in size. In winter time, this may be overnight or 12 hours, be patient! Alternatively you can prove the croissants in a 25-30°C (77-86°F) oven, taking care not to melt the butter if the temperature rises about 35°C (95°F).

BAKE: Preheat your oven to 200°C (400°F) 30 minutes prior to baking. Place the trays on the middle rack of the oven. Once the croissants are in the oven immediately, reduce the oven to 180°C (350°F). Bake for 10-15 minutes until golden brown.

COOL: Take croissants out of the oven and cool the croissants on a wire rack for 5 minutes before eating!

Croissants

ALMOND CROISSANT

I love almond croissants but I only eat my own because I don't like the almond custard filling most commercial almond croissants have. Also, I don't like the harsh fragrance of artificial butter almond essence. This almond frangipani filling satiates my craving for almond croissant. Do try and find the amaretto liquor I used to fragrant this frangipani mixture.

INGREDIENTS

One quantity of sourdough croissant dough

ALMOND FRANGIPANI
100g (3½oz) butter, soft
90g (3oz) whole almond, crushed roughly in a food processor

90g (3oz) blanched almond or whole almond, crushed finely to an almond meal consistency
150g (5oz) icing sugar
1½ tablespoons potato flour
2 tablespoons amaretto liquor or 1 tablespoon vanilla bean paste

METHOD

Using the 'pulse' button, blend the ingredients for almond frangipani in a food processor until mixed well. Do not over-process or the mixture will become an oily paste

SHAPE
Proceed as per plain croissant making up to 10 medium or 16 small croissants.

Place 30–50g (1–1 ¾oz) of almond frangipani on the base of the triangle.

Starting from this filled side, roll up the triangle once then pinch each side of the almond filling before rolling the rest of the triangle, making sure the almond frangipani is encased in the centre to prevent leakage of almond frangipani as it bakes.

If you like, using a pastry brush, you can egg-wash your almond croissants then sprinkle some slivered almonds or almond flakes on top.

For rising and baking follow as directed for plain croissants.

Pain au Chocolat

PAIN AU CHOCOLAT

Pain au chocolat is just another name for a chocolate-filled croissant. The traditional shape is a rectangular roll of croissant dough filled with chocolate baton made up of chocolate, butter and liquor. The are difficult to find—almost all of the available chocolate batons are made of compound chocolate. So, either use chocolate buttons or chop up your chocolate block of couverture chocolate. I prefer 55 per cent dark couverture chocolate, but chocolate is such a personal thing, it is up to you!

INGREDIENTS

One quantity of sourdough croissant
500g (17½oz) dark or milk couverture

chocolate baton or buttons (you can also cut long pieces of a block of chocolate

METHOD

SHAPE

Roll your croissant dough into a rectangle measuring 30 x 80cm (12 x 32ins), then cut the dough in half vertically into two 15 x 80cm (6 x 32ins) halves.

Measure 8–10cm (3.2–4ins) vertically to give you eight or ten rectangles measuring 8 x 15cm (3.2 x 6ins) or 10 x 15cm (4 x 6ins).

Place 20–30g (²/₃–1oz) of chocolate buttons or baton on one side of the shorter side, just as you would make sushi.

Starting from this chocolate-filled side, roll up the rectangle carefully, making sure the chocolate is encased in the centre to prevent leakage of melting chocolate as it bakes.

For rising and baking follow as directed for plain croissants.

Pain au Chocolat

Tarte Tatin

TARTE TATIN

Tarte Tartin is essentially a French version of an upside-down apple tart; here I use my sourdough croissant dough as the pastry, because it produces mroe softness and crumb for the caramel to cling to. Traditionally, puff or flaky pastry is used here.

INGREDIENTS

Half quantity of sourdough croissant

CARAMEL
200g (7oz) organic raw sugar
150g (5oz) organic butter

FRUIT
6 medium-sized organic apples (you can also use pears, bananas or one small pineapple, depending on size)
Juice of half a lemon to prevent browning of apples or pear once cut

METHOD

CARAMELISE SUGAR: Use a 24cm-round (9.6in), deep heavy cast-iron sauté pan (6–7.5cm/2.5in deep), non-stick pan is preferable. Smear butter on the base of the pan then scatter the sugar on top of the butter. Slowly melt the sugar and then bring to the boil. Reduce the heat, and, without stirring, continue cooking until you get a slightly lighter than golden brown caramel, taking care not to burn. Do not stir or you will crystallise the sugar. Let caramel cool a little, while you prepare the apples.

PREPARE APPLES: Peel and cut apples or pears in half, then remove the core. Place the apple halves in water, acidulated with the lemon juice. Drain well on paper towel. Arrange on top of the caramel in the pan, cut sides up. Pack them close together, as the fruit will shrink as it cooks. Continue cooking for about 20 minutes until just cooked but not mushy and the liquid is reduced by half. Let cool a little, while you roll the dough.

PREHEAT YOUR OVEN TO 225°C (437°F)

ROLL THE DOUGH AND PREPARE FOR FINAL ASSEMBLY: Roll the dough to about 5–7mm (2–2 ½in) thickness (depending how you like it) and cut out a 25cm-wide (10in) circle. Make sure your pastry circle is about 1cm (½in) larger than tarte tatin pan. Carefully fold the pastry in four to form an envelope and carefully lift it into the pan. Unfold the pastry to cover the fruit, tucking the edges around the rim of the pan.

BAKE: Bake the tarte tatin for 5 minutes at 225°C (437°F). Reduce the heat to 205°C (400°F) and bake for another 15–20 minutes, until the pastry is golden brown. Put a large plate on top of the pan and very carefully invert the tarte tatin. You must invert the tarte tatin out of the pan immediately or the caramel will stick onto the pan. Pour excess caramel over the top. Enjoy with a huge dollop of organic cream or crème fraiche.

SUITABLE FOR FREEZING AND WILL KEEP FOR A COUPLE OF MONTHS FROZEN.

CINNAMON 'N' RAISIN SCROLLS OR ESCARGOT

Most escargots are pastry scrolls filled with custard and rum-soaked sultanas. The filling for this recipe is inspired by my student and lovely friend, Cathie, who hand-makes traditional, yeasted organic butter croissants and pastries to sell at farmers' markets. I find using the cinnamon-sugar-butter mixture, instead of custard, gives you the same sweet satisfaction but a much lighter taste (so you can eat another one).

INGREDIENTS

One quantity of sourdough croissant dough
500g (13oz) raw sugar
75g (2½oz) softened butter
2–3 heaped teaspoons organic ground

cinnamon
250–400g (9–14oz) of raisins or sultanas
soaked in 50g (1¾oz) of rum for 2 hours,
then drained

METHOD

Blitz together sugar, butter and cinnamon in a food processor.

SHAPE: Cut the dough into two halves. On a lightly floured surface, roll each dough piece into a square of 40 x 40cm (16ins). For each half, sprinkle as much or as little of the cinnamon/sugar mixture. Make sure the cinnamon sugar filling is evenly distributed. Press the filling into the dough with your rolling pin. Roll up the rectangle into a tight log, from the filled part towards the unfilled quarter. Wrap each log in plastic wrap and freeze for about 45 minutes until reasonably firm, so that it is easy to cut. Allow the log to rest at room temperature for 15 minutes before cutting. Cut the logs into 3cm (1 ¼in) slices then lay the slices spiral side down onto the two baking sheets, allow space in between scrolls as they will expand. Sprinkle more cinnamon sugar and scatter the soaked sultanas, taking care to distribute the filling evenly. For rising and baking follow as directed for plain croissants.

Cinnamon 'N' Raisin Scrolls or Escargot

Sourdough Stollen

CAKES AND CELEBRATORY BREADS

SOURDOUGH STOLLEN

Stollen is a dense and fragrant cake. Dresden, Germany, is considered the spiritual home of this festive bread. It is the symbol of baby Jesus's blanket, while the coloured fruits represent the gift of the Magi. Stollen dough is a yeasted or sourdough 'shortbread' dough. It keeps well because of its low moisture content and high proportion of butter, sugar and a generous coating of icing sugar. Stollen is made in the cold winter months. I would recommend machine kneading, as the kneading process is long and arduous!

INGREDIENTS

FRUIT MIXTURE: PREPARE THIS MIXTURE THE DAY BEFORE YOU PLAN TO MAKE THE STOLLEN DOUGH.

ONE STOLLEN	TWO STOLLEN	
115g (4oz)	225g (8oz)	small dark raisins (muscat) or sultanas
35g (1¼oz)	75g (2½oz)	candied peels (candied orange and candied citron)
2 tablespoons	4 tablespoons	amaretto (bitter almond liqueur)
2 tablespoons	4 tablespoons	cointreau (orange liqueur)

Mix well and marinate all above ingredients at least overnight.

WHOLE ALMOND MARZIPAN

ONE STOLLEN	TWO STOLLEN	
100g (3½oz)	200g (7oz)	butter, softened
175g (6oz)	350g (12oz)	whole almonds
150g (5oz)	300g (10½oz)	icing sugar or raw caster sugar
1½ tablespoons	3 tablespoons	potato flour
1½ tablespoons	3 tablespoons	amaretto liquor

Put all ingredients into your food processor. Use several pulses to blitz the mixture until it forms a paste (it will be slightly sticky). Knead briefly by hand but do not over-process or your mixture will be oily. Refrigerate in-between uses—it should keep for a month in a cold fridge or can be frozen for up to three months.

DOUGH INGREDIENTS

ONE STOLLEN	TWO STOLLEN	
125g (4oz)	250g (9oz)	butter, softened and at room temperature
65g (2oz)	125g (4oz)	caster or icing sugar
1 teaspoon	2 teaspoons	salt
300g (10½oz)	600g (21oz)	unbleached white wheat/spelt flour (high gluten)
150g (5oz)	300g (10½oz)	white sourdough starter
25g (¾oz)	50g (1¾oz)	organic milk or soy milk
1	2	eggs
2–3 teaspoons	1½–2 tablespoons	amaretto (optional)

METHOD

MEASURE INGREDIENTS (2–3 MINS): Use, preferably, a digital scale, to weigh the butter, sugar and salt. Put these ingredients in a bowl.

MIX AND BEAT (5 MINS): Beat butter, sugar and salt until light and fluffy. Keep cool but not chilled.

MEASURE INGREDIENTS (2–3 MINS): Use, preferably, a digital scale, to weigh the rest of the ingredients. Put all ingredients in a non-metallic bowl, starting with the starter and milk then the rest of the ingredients and lastly the salt.

MIX INGREDIENTS (2–3 MINS): Using a spatula or a wooden spoon, stir the ingredients together until they form a cohesive mass. Add the butter/sugar mixture to the dough mixture. Mix well until you have a homogeneous crumbly dough mixture.

Using your dough mixer with the K beater (or paddle), mix and knead for about 5 minutes until the dough comes together. Rest the dough for 20 minutes to let the gluten develop. The mixture will look like cookie dough, dry and crumbly at this stage, but do not worry!

REST (15–20 MINS): Rest the dough in the bowl for 15–20 minutes.

KNEADING (20–25 MINS): You can knead this dough normally as it is fairly dry, so it won't stick to your hands or the bench.

ALTERNATIVELY

USING A ROTARY MIXER

Using your rotary mixer, switch the paddle to the dough hook. Knead for 5 minutes, on a medium speed, making sure the dough does not cling to the paddle. Increase the speed of the mixer if the dough clings to the paddle. Rest the dough again for another 20 minutes. This 'knead and rest' method provides a chance for the gluten to develop, preventing the dough becoming hot, as well as preventing the dough mixer motor from burning out. Do this 5 minute knead followed with a 20 minute rest two more times (three times total). Repeat this process until your dough becomes shiny and elastic—the dough may look oily or some butter oil may squeeze out from the dough (this is caused by the heat generated from the vigorous kneading).

ADD: Add in marinated fruits. Knead and mix well to evenly distribute.

DIVIDE THE DOUGH (5 MINS): Divide the dough into two, if you are doing the double recipe. The single recipe will make one stollen. This stollen will be bigger than a commercially made stollen which is 500g (17 ½oz) in weight. I prefer to make the double recipe, which will make two large stollens or three smaller stollens. Let the dough sit for 5 minutes to relax the gluten.

SHAPE THE DOUGH (10 MINS): Using the whole almond marzipan, make a log measuring 25cm (10ins) long and 3-4cm (1–1 ½ins) in diameter. Roll each stolllen dough into an oval shape of 30cm (12in) long and 1.25cm (½in) thick, leaving the outer edges slightly thicker. Lay the marzipan log horizontally about one-third of the way through the oval shaped dough. Proceed to enclose the marzipan log with the dough by rolling it tightly into the dough. Roll away until you have used up two-thirds of the dough width. Tuck the edges of the rolled dough into the remaining one-third of the dough underneath. Very carefully bend the edges of the stollen to form a slight crescent shape. Lift the stollen onto a sheet of baking paper.

SECOND/FINAL RISE (4-8 HOURS): Rise the stollen until about one and a half times its size, at a comfortable room temperature around 20–25°C (68–77°F). Make sure the dough is covered or mist with water to prevent drying. The dough will spread a little.

BAKE: Bake in a hot oven, preheated to 205°C (401°F) for about 7-8 minutes, then reduce the oven to 175°C (349°F) for a further 25-30 minutes until browned and cooked. These loaves will look dark brown when cooked. If you are unsure whether the loaves have cooked through, turn the oven off, and let the loaves sit in the oven for a further 10 minutes. Remove loaves from oven, taking care not to burn yourself! As the stollen comes out of the oven, brush generously with melted ghee or butter mixed with a liqueur of your choice (I recommend a mixture of Amaretto and Cointreau). Dust heavily with icing sugar (use a flour sifter).

COOL AND STORE: Let the stollen cool completely before cutting/eating, allowing at least 2–3 hours. Stollen is best eaten within two weeks of baking as it will dry out a little. Stollen will keep well wrapped tightly in waxed paper and aluminium foil. Leave it in the coolest part of your house and it should keep well for a month or two.

SUITABLE FOR FREEZING AND WILL KEEP FOR UP TO THREE MONTHS FROZEN.

Sourdough Stollen cross-section

Orange-flavoured Sourdough Challah

ORANGE-FLAVOURED SOURDOUGH CHALLAH

MAKES 1 CHALLAH

I love challah, a traditional Jewish celebratory bread because it has a lighter texture and fewer calories than brioche. Traditionally, the fat used in challah is oil rather than butter, because challah is dairy-free, for religious reasons. I have added grated orange rind and candied orange, which marry well with the flavour of challah. I make this challah once a week in winter, when my huge orange trees are full of ripe oranges. I never buy commercial candied orange peel as it is full of preservatives. Candied peels are very easy and quick to make at home when oranges are plentiful (there is a fabulous recipe for candied orange peels in my first book). This dough rises well and will give you a large and impressive challah for a Sabbath dinner.

INGREDIENTS

100g (3½oz) active white wheat or spelt
   sourdough starter
230g (8oz) filtered water
100g (3½oz) yoghurt
113g (4oz) egg yolks (best) or whole eggs
50–80g (1¾–2 ½oz) raw organic sugar
535g (19oz) white spelt or wheat flour

50g (1¾oz) macadamia, grapeseed or
   softened/melted butter
2 teaspoons sea-salt
1 tablespoon grated orange rinds
65g (2oz) candied orange peels, preferably
   homemade

METHOD

MEASURE INGREDIENTS(2–3 MINS): Use, preferably, a digital scale, to weigh all ingredients. Put all ingredients, except grated orange rinds and candied peels, in a non-metallic bowl, starting with water, starter and honey, then the rest of the ingredients and lastly the salt.

MIX INGREDIENTS (2–3 MINS): Using a spatula or a wooden spoon, stir the ingredients together until they form a cohesive mass.

REST (15–20 MINS)

KNEADING –AIR KNEADING (15–20 MINS): Using your fingertips, throw your dough into the air and then slap/throw it onto your bench. After you have done this for about 5 minutes, the dough will have developed some elasticity and should be soft and elastic, but not wet. Knead in the oil/softened butter to distribute well into the dough. Continue kneading for an extra 10-15 minutes. This dough, like a brioche dough benefits from a long kneading to give it a fine crumb.

DO THE WINDOW PANE TEST: See 'Sourdough Bread Making Step-by-Step'.

ADD AND DISTRIBUTE (5 MINS): Add both grated orange rinds and candied orange peels. Knead well to distribute these two ingredients.

FIRST RISE ABOUT (2-3 HOURS OR YOU CAN RETARD THIS DOUGH COVERED IN THE FRIDGE OVERNIGHT): Gather your dough together and shape into a ball, let it rest in a covered non-metallic container or a bowl covered with a wet tea towel or a wet cling wrap. Let your dough rise to about one and a quarter times its size—the time taken will vary.

DIVIDE AND SHAPE (20 MINS): Divide the dough into four equal pieces (about 250g (9oz)) or three equal pieces (about 340g (12oz)). Oil your hands and bench with the smallest amount of oil if dough feels slightly sticky. If you use too much oil, it will be too slippery to roll your dough. Shape each piece by rolling it into a log, rest for about 10 minutes. Roll each piece of dough into a 30cm (12inches) long rope. Taper both ends of each rope. Starting from one tapered end, braid the strands. Stretch the dough more towards the end of the braid so that it comes to more of a point. Pinch the strands together at the end of the braid. Using both hands, push the ends together so that the challah loaf is about 35 x 10cm (14 x 4ins) wide. Place the loaf on a piece of non-stick baking paper.

SECOND/FINAL RISE ABOUT (4-8 HOURS): You can glaze with an egg-wash or milk and sprinkle with sugar crystals or candied peels if you wish and cover. Rise again until almost doubled, about 4-8 hours at a comfortable room temperature, around 20–25°C (68–77°F), make sure the dough is covered or mist with water to prevent drying. The dough will rise up as well as spread its width, do not worry. It is very difficult to do an indentation test with this type of dough, as it doesn't bounce back much at all. So observe the increase size of the dough rather than the indentation test. The dough will puff up and increase its height another 25 per cent in the oven.

BAKE: Bake in a hot oven, preheated to 215°C (420°F) for about 10 minutes, then reduce the oven to 185°C (365°F) for a further 30-35 minutes until dark brown and cooked. If you are unsure whether the loaves have cooked through, turn the oven off, and let the loaves sit in the oven for a further 10 minutes. Remove loaves from oven, taking care not to burn yourself!

SOURDOUGH CHRISTMAS CAKE

MAKES 1 CAKE

This is a gorgeous, spicy, fruity Christmas cake. I have changed this recipe slightly from how it appeared in my first book to make a lighter, moister cake full of fruits. The cake batter will now ferment and rise for a long 6 hours, or overnight in winter time. The long fermentation allows pre-digestion of gluten, fat and sugar.

INGREDIENT

PART 1: FRUIT AND LIQUEUR MIXTURE (PREPARE THIS MIXTURE AT LEAST 12 HOURS BEFORE YOU PLAN TO MAKE THE CAKE)

500–600g (21oz) dried fruits of your choice, larger fruits need to be chopped to a sultana size

100g (3½oz) nuts of your choice, chopped

(optional)

100g (3½oz) brandy, whisky or any other liqueur of your liking, or apple juice

Mix well and marinate all of the above ingredients overnight, minimum. If you can plan ahead, marinating the fruits and nuts for a longer time (one to four weeks) is even better. Make sure that you drain any liquid before mixing with the cake.

PART 2: FLOUR AND SPICE MIXTURE

250g (9oz) organic unbleached white wheat or spelt flour (plain or cake flour)

2 teaspoons (5g) mixed spice

½ teaspoon ground cinnamon

½ teaspoon ground ginger or cloves

Sift together all ingredients a couple of times, set aside.

PART 3: CAKE MIXTURE

250g (9oz) organic butter, softened and at room temperature

100g (3½oz) rapadura sugar or brown sugar

300g (10½oz) raw caster sugar

1 teaspoon vanilla extract

6 organic eggs, at room temperature

150g (5oz) grated apple (peeled first)

50g (1¾oz) molasses

500g (17½oz) white sourdough starter

50g (1¾oz) flour, extra

METHOD

MEASURE INGREDIENTS(2–3 MINS): Use, preferably, a digital scale, to weigh all ingredients.

MIX INGREDIENTS (2–3 MINS): In a warmed bowl, cream butter and sugar until light and fluffy. Slowly add the eggs, one by one. The mixture will look curdled at this stage, but do not worry! Add the extra flour and grated apple, mix well. Using a spatula or low-speed mixer, add the starter and molasses. In a separate bowl, add the fruits to the sifted flour and spices mixture. Mix well until the fruits are coated with flour. This will make sure the fruits are well distributed in the cake. Add the fruits and flour mixture into the butter mixture. Using a spatula, mix well to distribute the fruit and nuts evenly.

FIRST AND FINAL RISE: Butter and line the cake tins with thick baking paper. Divide the cake mixture into two round cake tins (20cm (8ins) in diameter) or four 12.5cm–round (5ins) cake tins or 20 medium-sized muffin tins (125g (4oz) each). A 20cm-round cake tin will hold 1kg (36oz) of cake mixture and a 12.5cm-round cake tin will hold 500g (17 ½oz) of cake mixture. Ferment the dough for approximately 6 hours or overnight (in winter time). The dough will increase to about one and a half times its original size.

COOK THE CAKE:

PREHEAT YOUR OVEN TO 165ºC (329ºF)

BAKING FOR MUFFIN-SIZED CAKE OR 12.5CM-ROUND (5INS) CAKE: Place on lower third rack and bake for 45-50 minutes (muffin size) or approximately 1 hour 15 minutes for cake. Use a bamboo skewer to test if the cake is cooked in the middle (the bamboo skewer will come out clean).

FOR 20CM-ROUND CAKE: Place on lower third rack and bake for 45 minutes. Reduce heat to 150°C (302°F) and bake for another 1 hour to 1 ½ hours until golden brown. If the top of the cake browns too quickly, cover with aluminium foil. Use a bamboo skewer to test if the cake is cooked in the middle (the bamboo skewer will come out clean). Once the cakes are out of the oven, brush generously with a liqueur of your choice. Repeat this process several times in the next month. This will ensure the cake is moist, develops its complex taste, and prolongs its keeping quality. This cake is best eaten after a month or two as it will develop its complex flavour. It will keep well wrapped tightly in waxed paper and aluminium foil, and left it in the coolest part of your house. Alternatively, it will keep well in the fridge or freezer for three months.

Sourdough Christmas Cake

Sourdough Fig Upside-down Pudding Cake

SOURDOUGH FIG UPSIDE-DOWN PUDDING CAKE

MAKES 1 CAKE

When I lived in Fitzroy, Melbourne many moons ago, I used to go to a café on Smith Street to have a slice of their delicious pineapple upside-down cake. It was the inspiration for this cake. The consistency is between a pudding and a cake. You can substitute apple, rhubarb, quince, banana or even pineapple instead of fig. This cake looks spectacular and is delicious with a dollop of ice cream or crème fraiche.

INGREDIENTS

CAKE
475g (16oz) white/milk starter
    (6-12 hours prior to making the cake, mix
    25g (¾oz) any active starter you have, 250g
    (9oz) milk, 200g (7oz) white wheat/spelt,
    ferment until bubbly)
115g (4oz) sugar
2 large eggs
80g (2½oz) thick sour cream
1 teaspoon vanilla extract

¾ teaspoon baking soda
½ teaspoon ground cardamom
1 teaspoon salt

CARAMEL
200g (7oz) organic raw sugar
100g (3½oz) organic butter

FIGS
10 large figs

METHOD

CARAMELISE SUGAR: Use a 24cm-round (9.5 inch) deep heavy cast-iron sauté pan (6-7.5cm (2.5 inches) deep), non-stick pan is preferable. Smear butter on the base of the pan then scatter the sugar on top of the butter. Slowly melt the sugar, then bring to the boil. Reduce the heat, and, without stirring, continue cooking until you get a slightly darker than golden brown caramel, taking care not to burn your caramel. Do not stir or you will crystallise the sugar. Let caramel cool a little, while you prepare the fruits.

MAKE THE CAKE BATTER: Weigh all cake ingredients and put into the bowl. Beat the thick frothy mixture with a spatula or low-speed mixer and mix well.

PREHEAT YOUR OVEN TO 225°C (437°F)

PREPARE FRUITS: For figs, take off the stalks and cut in half vertically. Arrange the fig halves on top of the caramel in the pan, cut sides up. Pack them close together, as the fruit will shrink as it cooks. Continue cooking for about 10 minutes until the figs are just cooked but not mushy. Carefully pour the dough into the caramelised figs.

BAKE: Put the cake in the middle rack of the oven and immediately reduce the heat to 180°C (350°F) and bake for another 40–45 minutes, until the cake is golden brown. To test if it is done, insert a sharp bamboo skewer into the cake. If it comes out clean, then the cake is cooked. If crumb sticks to the skewer, leave cake in the oven for another 5–10 minutes. Put a large plate on top of the pan and invert the cake very, very carefully. You must invert the cake out of the pan immediately or the caramel will stick onto the pan. Pour excess caramel over the top. Enjoy with a huge dollop of vanilla ice-cream, cream or crème fraiche.

See also Gluten-Free Sourdough.

THINGS TO GO WITH SOURDOUGH

OLIVE & BASIL TAPENADE

This summer I had such a bountiful crop of basil-I harvested over five kilos of basil leaves. This recipe was inspired by my foodie friend, Mal. According to him, this green olive basil tapenade originates from the Basque in France. This recipe is my take on his description of how he makes this tapenade (I added the capers, parmesan and roasted the garlic). Luckily, he did say that my version is better than his, a great compliment from one of the best cooks I know!

You can use this tapenade as a delicious alternative to basil pesto, tossed through hot pasta for those of you who are allergic to nuts. I also use this as an accompaniment to grilled meat, chicken, fish or vegetables. For a standby meal, I often add a can of tuna into this tapenade, warmed slightly, then tossed into hot spaghetti. Delicious! NOTE: You can also use pitted kalamata olives for a vibrant, dark purple tapenade.

INGREDIENTS

125g (4oz) freshest basil leaves
125g (4oz) extra virgin olive oil
250g (9oz) pitted green olives, in oil
2–3 small chillies, seeded (optional)
2 heaped teaspoons capers

50–75g (1¾–2½oz) roasted garlic
75g (2½oz) parmesan or pecorino cheese, grated

METHOD

Chop basil leaves roughly in a food processor for a few seconds, using pulsing actions, until they are roughly chopped. Add half of the olive oil and pulse a couple more times to mix. Do not over process the basil leaves to form a paste. Remove chopped basil to a medium size bowl. Pulse the olives, chilli and capers together, using your food processor, until they form a coarse paste. Tip the olive and caper coarse paste onto the chopped basil, add the remaining oil and grated parmesan and mix well. This tapenade will keep in the fridge for a week or two. Enjoy!

ROASTED RED PEPPER & WALNUT DIP

This has to be my most favourite dip ever! It is also great as a spread for toast or crackers, as well as a sauce for roasted or char-grilled lamb or chicken. This dip originally comes from Aleppo, Syria. The principal ingredients are usually fresh roasted peppers, ground walnuts, breadcrumbs, and olive oil. This is my version. If you prefer a coarser dip, process peppers and walnuts independently. Mix well with the remaining ingredients in a bowl, until all ingredients are well distributed.

INGREDIENTS

3 large red red peppers (capsicums)
125g (4oz) walnuts, shelled and roughly chopped
90g (3oz) lightly toasted fresh sourdough breadcrumbs
2–3 garlic cloves, fresh or lightly roasted
15–30g (½–1 oz) pomegranate molasses
125ml (4fl oz) lemon juice
1 tablespoon hot water

1 tablespoon maple syrup or agave syrup
60ml (2fl oz) extra virgin olive oil
1 teaspoon sea-salt
¼–½ teaspoon roasted dry chilli or dry chilli (crushed) or chilli powder
¼–½ teaspoon smoked paprika (pimentos) (optional)
½ teaspoon ground cummin seeds

METHOD

Roast the red peppers in a 200ºC (400ºF) oven for 15-20 minutes or on a low naked flame (I do mine on top of my gas stove burner) using silicone tongs, until they are blackened and charred evenly. You need to move the peppers around continuously. Put charred peppers inside a glass bowl and close with a lid to sweat. This will soften the skin, making it easier to peel. Once cooled enough to handle, peel away charred skin and remove membrane, seeds and stalks. Resist the temptation to wash the peppers with water as this will remove some of the smoky flavour. Instead, run your fingers under tap water if the charred skins and seeds stick to your fingers. Roughly pulse all ingredients in your food processor. Do not over-process at this stage—a coarse paste consistency is what you need to achieve. Check seasonings and adjust to taste. Let the dip rest for a few hours or overnight in the fridge for the flavour to blend and mellow. Serve with crisp sourdough crackers or bread.

Olive & Basil Tapenade

Roasted Red Pepper & Walnut Dip

Tomato & Passionfruit Jam

Yoke's Unconventional Basil Pesto

TOMATO & PASSIONFRUIT JAM

This gorgeous recipe was given to me by my student and friend, Bianca, another brilliant cook. Thank you Bianca for allowing me to include this recipe in this book. I have adapted her original recipe and used lemon juice instead of tartaric acid to do the gelling job, and it works just as well sans the harsh arftertaste..

INGREDIENTS

1.5kg (53oz) red tomatoes (under-ripe and hard are the best)

1kg (36oz) sugar

60ml (2fl oz) lemon juice or ½ teaspoon tartaric acid

190g (6½oz) passionfruit pulp, including the seeds

METHOD

Boil 4-5 litres (135–169fl oz) of water in a large pot. Cut a cross on the base of each tomato. Scald the tomatoes in the boiling water until they start to burst and their skins peel away. Remove the tomatoes from the boiling water with a slotted spoon. Discard the water. Remove skins and chop the tomatoes roughly. In a large, heavy shallow pot or roasting pan, place tomatoes and sugar. Slowly bring to a rapid boil. Continue to boil for 30 minutes. Stir well and regularly. Add lemon juice and passionfruit pulp, and continue to boil for another 15 minutes or until the mixture thickens and starts to gel.

DO A GEL TEST: Spoon a little jam onto a well-chilled saucer and put it in the freezer for a minute. Push the edge of the jam with your finger. If it wrinkles, then your jam is ready. If not, put jam back on heat and keep boiling for another 5–10 minutes. Repeat the test until it reaches this setting stage. When the jam is ready, carefully ladle into sterilised jars and seal straight away while still hot.

YOKE'S UNCONVENTIONAL BASIL PESTO

This pesto is totally unconventional-so apologies to the Genovese! However, I make no apology for how good this pesto tastes. I use this pesto for everything, even as a spread on toast!

INGREDIENTS

150g (5oz) freshest basil leaves
250g (9oz) olive oil
500g (17½oz) mixed nuts of your choice (I use pine, macadamia, walnut, almond, pecan and Brazilian nuts)

50–75g (1¾–2½oz) roasted garlic, peeled
175g (6oz) parmesan or pecorino cheese, chopped into small cubes
25g (¾oz) sea salt or to taste

METHOD

Chop basil leaves in a food processor for a few seconds, using pulsing actions, until they are roughly chopped. Add half of the olive oil and pulse a couple more times to mix. Do not over process the basil leaves to form a paste. Remove chopped basil to a medium size bowl. Crush all nuts in a food processor for a few seconds, using pulsing actions, until they are roughly crushed. Do not over-crush the nuts to form a paste. Remove nuts onto the bowl with the chopped basil leaves. Pulse the roasted garlic, cheese and sea salt together, until they become coarsely chopped. Tip the garlic cheese mixture into the bowl with nuts and basil leaves, add the olive oil and mix well. Enjoy.

PLUM PASTE

This chapter would not be complete without something sweet to accompany bread. Luckily for me, I was given this gorgeous 'jewel-like', intensely plumy, plum paste by one of my students, Moira. Thank you Moira for sharing this recipe! You can use this as a spread or as an accompaniment to cheese (as an alternative to quince paste). It is absolutely necessary to use slightly under-ripe plums. They have a higher pectin level, which helps the paste set well.

INGREDIENTS

1kg (36oz) plums, slightly under ripe and
   washed
250g (9oz) water

Caster sugar (for quantity see method below)
40ml (1fl oz) lemon juice

METHOD

Line a 28 x 18cm (11 x 7 inch) tin with baking paper across the base and up the two long sides. Remove the stalks, and any blemishes from the plums. In a heavy-based saucepan, add plums to water and simmer until they completely soften. Strain the cooked plums to remove the skin and seeds, pushing the pulp through a sieve. Weigh the plum pulp and put it back into the saucepan. Add an equal quantity of sugar to the plum pulp. Mix pulp with sugar, then bring back to boil. Stir well to completely dissolve the sugar. Add lemon juice into the plum mixture. Keep this on a brisk simmer for 30 minutes, stirring occasionally to prevent sticking. Skim off any scum at about 25 minutes.

DO A GEL TEST: Spoon a little jam onto a well-chilled saucer and put it in the freezer for a minute. Push the edge of the paste mixture with your finger. If it wrinkles, then your paste is ready. If not, put paste back on heat and keep boiling for another 5–10 minutes. Repeat the test until it reaches this setting stage.

Carefully pour into prepared tin and refrigerate. Cut into squares/rectangles, wrap each piece in baking paper and store in an airtight container in the fridge. It will last several months.

Plum Paste

ACKNOWLEDGEMENTS

My first and foremost gratitude is for all my students and readers all over the world who have generously supported me through my first book, *Wild Sourdough* and my classes. Without you, this book would never have been created. Thank you for your kind words and numerous questions, they helped me enormously to be a better baker, writer and teacher.

To my gorgeous daughter, Dechen, thank you for your unconditional love, wisdom, insights, and endless patience. You are my light!

To my dad 'Papi', thank you for making me a strong and resilient person, knowing you are in my life makes me never ever give up.

To my mum 'Mami', thank you giving me your intelligence, your amazing ability to be a 'bridge', and of course, your baking gene.

My endless gratitude to my uncle, Kiu Ing, for loving me and supporting me all my life.

A very special thank you to Janet for allowing me to use your house for the photographs and your generous hospitality.

Thank you so much to my students and dear friends, Tania, Janet, Leah and Belinda for proofing my recipes; Bianca and Moira for sharing the plum paste and tomato and passionfruit recipes.

A very big thank you for Sonia and Shaun for your endless hours editing my manuscripts.

Graeme, my deepest thank you for your love and support to me and Dechen—I wouldn't have started this sourdough career without you in my life.

Dhillon, thank you for always turning my light switch back on! You always miraculously appear whenever I need you.

My infinite gratitude to Shaun, for your love, generosity, support and kindness. Thank you for the lessons, to know what I needed to fight for.

To Leah, Sonia, Jenny and Dean, my dear friends, thank you for your friendship, relentless help and support.

My sincere gratefulness to my photographer Alan, my wonderful editor Jodi, my publishing manager Lliane, my publisher Linda and my book designer Celeste.

And a very special thank you to everyone in my life, you know who you are. I would not be the person I am today without all of you.

Lastly, to the divine, my deepest gratitude for showing me over and over again that I always have what I need ... in abundance.

ABOUT THE AUTHOR

Following successful careers in fashion and finance, Yoke Mardewi took the plunge and decided to work at her first love and passion—the making and sharing of food, in particular, sourdough bread making.

Her first book *Wild Sourdough:the natural way to bake* was an introduction to sourdough bread making and quickly became a much loved practical textbook on sourdough bread making. This second book extends the art to encompass many of the issues and ideas raised by her students and readers. These include soft sourdough, whole-rye, croissants and pastry, and gluten-free breads.

Yoke continues to run sourdough bread making cooking classes on both the West and East coasts of Australia. She welcomes opportunities to teach anywhere else in the world. Her classes are as much about sharing her warmth and passion for life as they are about the joy of food.

She features regularly in food and health magazines, newspapers and websites. Her own website, www.wildsourdough.com.au, has grown to include information about her classes, an on-line ordering for her signed books and starters (both rye and gluten free), a sourdough FAQ's and Yoke's blog.

She is a strong supporter of organic/ biodynamic farming.

Yoke currently lives in Perth with her daughter and two jack russells.

She supports and encourages others to have the courage to pursue their passion in life. She still believes in miracles and random act of kindness.

Yoke welcomes contact from all her students and readers around the world.
Email: yoke@wildsourdough.com.au
Website: www.wildsourdough.com.au

INDEX

First published in Australia in 2011 by New Holland Publishers (Australia) Pty Ltd

Sydney • Auckland • London • Cape Town

1/66 Gibbes Street, Chatswood NSW 2067 Australia

www.newholland.com.au

218 Lake Road Northcote Auckland 0746 New Zealand

86 Edgware Road London W2 2EA United Kingdom

80 McKenzie Street Cape Town 8001 South Africa

A record of this book is available from the National Library of Australia.

ISBN 9781742571317

Publisher: Linda Williams

Publishing Manager: Lliane Clarke

Project Editor: Jodi De Vantier

Designer: Celeste Vlok

Food Photography: Yoke Mardewi and Alan Macdonald

Food Styling: Yoke Mardewi

Printer: Everbest Printing Co. Ltd